The Long Slog

These articles originally appeared in *The Week Behind* and are reproduced with both thanks and acknowledgment.
http://www.theweekbehind.com

Library of Congress Cataloging-in-Publication Data

Jacobs, Scott, 1950–

The Long Slog
A Funny Thing Happened On The Way To The White House
by Stump Connolly

Includes Index.

1. Politics 2. Media I. Title

ISBN: 1-879652-00-5
EAN13: 9781879652002

First Edition 2009
Printed in the United States of America

 Dead Tree Press is an imprint of Subtle Communications. Distributed by First Flight Books, 2144 N. Hudson, Chicago, IL 60614.

www.deadtreepress.com

The Long Slog

Stump Connolly

Dead Tree Press
Chicago

To Nick

"I've been running for 15 months now, which means there are babies who have been born and are now walking and talking since I started running for President."

— Barack Obama

Table of Contents

PART ONE

A Funny Thing Happened On The Way To The Nomination

PART TWO

Lipstick On A Pig

Preface

WHAT FOLLOWS ARE 43 columns I wrote along the campaign trail of a truly remarkable presidential race. The contest spanned nearly two years and cost over $1.7 billion. The winner, Barack Obama, spent $740 million alone, more than George Bush and John Kerry together spent only four years before.

Books will be written with all the inside information on how the Obama campaign transformed politics, and perhaps the nation. This is not one of them. Instead, it is a running commentary on what the race looked like from the eye of the storm.

By the very definition of journalism, these columns are a first draft of history. What I saw when I saw it. Most were written on the run as the campaign wound its way through the primary states, or sitting in coffee shops at the conventions, or, too often, in cheap motels against a fast-approaching deadline. That makes this also a very personal view of history composed of situations I sought out and people I met as an uninvited blogger along the campaign trail.

Presidential campaigns are a bubbling cauldron of competing interests with many cooks stirring the pot. The candidates, the handlers, the funders, the reporters, bloggers, pundits and, yes, the voters all influence the outcome. As I hope you'll see in these pages, they are real people, interesting people, who give up years of their lives to this oddly American enterprise.

The candidates run, and we run alongside trying to make sense of what they do and say. This quest takes us to some of the strangest precincts in the land. We talk to whoever comes across our radar. We read each other voraciously to see what the others have that we do not. We guess. We conjecture on what will happen. And we pontificate on why it didn't.

Politics is an imperfect science, and thus a perfect subject for political pundits. But it's also a lot of fun. So if you enjoy politics, pull up a chair and listen to my tale.

PART ONE

A Funny Thing Happened On The Way To The Nomination

Do The Math!

April 13, 2007

ARE WE HEADED to the first brokered political convention since 1952? Is it a possibility? Or a certainty? Do the math.

The scenarios are different for Republican and Democratic presidential candidates, but the rush of states to advance their 2008 presidential primaries to a Super Tuesday showdown on February 5 makes it more likely, not less, that no frontrunner can emerge with enough delegates to assure a first ballot victory at the party conventions.

What if, after New York, California, Illinois, New Jersey, Florida, Texas, Michigan and all the other states threatening to move up their primaries cast their ballots — and it's a split decision?

For the Democrats, it's a particularly touchy situation. Democratic party rules forbid winner-take-all primaries. State delegates are apportioned among contenders according to their share of the primary vote, provided a candidate receives at least 15 percent of the votes cast.

April 17, 2006

Former Alaskan Sen. Mike Gravel becomes first candidate to declare for presidency

December 28, 2006

John Edwards enters race

January 11, 2007

Ron Paul enters race

Chris Dodd enters race

January 20, 2007

Hillary Clinton enters race

So if three or more Democrats stay in the race through early February, even a big winner on Super Tuesday will have to struggle to turn his victory into an automatic nomination.

When the Democrats awaken after the February balloting, they will discover that 2,275 of their 4,362 convention delegates already have been selected. Let's assume the three leading contenders — Hillary Clinton, Barack Obama, and John Edwards — roll through these primaries with approximately the same poll numbers they garnered in a CBS Poll last March (36, 28 and 18 percent, respectively.) One can adjust out the other candidates who haven't reached the 15 percent threshold and conclude the delegate tallies on February 6 would look like this:

Hillary Clinton — 1,001 delegates
Barack Obama — 774 delegates
John Edwards — 500 delegates

On the surface, that might look like a decisive lead for Sen. Clinton (or whoever is holding that top spot come the actual race.) Alas, there are only 1,237 delegates left to be picked up in all the remaining primaries. If Sen. Clinton wants to go into the

Democratic convention assured of the majority (2,181 delegates*) needed to win the nomination, she will have to win 95 percent of the delegates up for grabs in the remaining primaries.

There is, of course, a grand (short) tradition in politics of Super Tuesday losers dropping out if a frontrunner can properly spank them on the big day. But we are presented this year with three candidates who have no incentive to give up so easily. All three will have campaign war chests large enough not only to pick and choose their races on Super Tuesday but to soldier on if there is no decisive winner. Even if Edwards can't rise above a third-place showing, he may be the least likely to leave an unfinished race, not only to vindicate his wife's devotion to the campaign as she battles terminal cancer, but to give her an opportunity to play a crucial role in a convention that may be as dramatic as any we've seen in our lifetime.

Not a lot needs to go wrong to see a divided convention. If all the campaigns stick to their game plans — and their game plan is right — the spread between the frontrunners will narrow, and the probability of a brokered convention will increase.

In the past, the news media has played a key role in creating momentum for the eventual nominee. Coverage of one primary sets the table with expectations for the next. Election night TV anchors like to anoint the winner — and drive the losers off the battlefield, but the media is hardly a monolith these days. It is divided into the mainstream media and the political blogosphere. And the candidates themselves have Internet operations this year that can, in a single email, spin a story that will reach more people than subscribe to the next day's *New York Times.*

January 28, 2007

Mike Huckabee enters race

January 31, 2007

Joe Biden enters race

February 10, 2007

Barack Obama enters race

February 13, 2007

Mitt Romney enters race

There is a subterfuge in these numbers. All the calculations are made without factoring in the 796 superdelegates who will automatically attend the convention as "unpledged" delegates by virtue of their position as governors, congressmen or members of the Democratic National Committee. Many already have or will soon endorse their favorite candidate (and it's only a matter of time before media websites start tracking them as well.)

If the Democratic race remains fluid after Super Tuesday, the superdelegates are free to change their minds at any point before or during the August 25 convention in Denver. They are, after all, the powerbrokers who will broker the convention should an impasse come about.

The Republican scenario is more complex, but no less intriguing. Republicans will take only 2,517 delegates to their Labor Day convention in Minneapolis. Some 662 (26 percent) will be officially unpledged. These include every state party chairmen, every Republican state committeeman and committeewoman, and, under more liberal Republican rules, delegations from states like Washington, Colorado, Nevada, and Maine who will go to the convention not bound to vote for any candidate.

If all the states planning to move up their primaries succeed, 1,444 Republican delegates will be selected by February 6. Eight of these early primary states apportion delegates, just as Democrats do, based on a candidate's percentage of the vote. Nine are winner-take-all states. The remaining five, including California, Florida, Georgia and Michigan, give three delegates to the winner in each Congressional district and some smaller percentage to the overall winner in the state.

It's not a great stretch to apply the same poll projection hypothesis to the Republicans as to the Democrats in these early primaries. No matter how poorly they fare in Iowa or New Hampshire, it's unlikely the top three Republicans — Rudy Giuliani, John McCain and Mitt Romney — will drop out before their home states of New York, Arizona and Massachusetts/Michigan vote. Each will have the war chest to compete nationally. Their only strategic problem will be figuring out which districts in which states can be effectively swayed by advertising and/or troops on the ground.

Time magazine published a poll in late March rating the top four Republican contenders. The results were:

Rudy Giuliani 35 percent
John McCain 22 percent
Newt Gingrich 12 percent
Mitt Romney 11 percent
Others 10 percent
Undecided 10 percent

February 14, 2007

Rudy Giuliani enters race

February 28, 2007

John McCain enters race

March 27, 2007

Time magazine poll

Republicans:

Giuliani 35%
McCain 22%
Gingrich 12%
Romney 11%
Huckabee 1%

Democrats:

Clinton 31%
Obama 24 %
Edwards 16%

Assuming Gingrich and Romney will not go down to the wire appealing to the same conservative base, and barring a breakaway start in Iowa and New Hampshire by one of the contenders, you can throw away the undecideds and calculate how a Giuliani, McCain and Romney/Gingrich (combined) race might look when the candidates wake up the morning after Super Tuesday.

If they divide the proportional-voting states in roughly the same manner as their current standings, and each takes a similar share of the winner-take-all Congressional districts, Giuliani will have 568 delegates (39.3 percent), McCain will have 455 (31.5 percent) and Romney/Gingrich will have 421 (29.2 percent) — nowhere near the 1,259 delegates needed to win the nomination.

The real problem is, because all those states have moved up, there are only 411 more delegates to be won in all the remaining primaries, caucuses and state conventions. A pack-leading Giuliani could win all of them and still be 280 delegates short of a majority.

The way the Republicans have written their rules the largest bloc of available votes by far at the convention will be party bosses and others chosen in state conventions by party leaders. California, the largest single state delegation, will have 173 votes. The vast block of unpledged superdelegates will have 662.

Donald Rumsfeld's axiom about known knowns, known unknowns and unknown unknowns applies to politics as well as Iraq. At this early stage, the "unknown unknowns" are spread across the playing field, chief among them being the existence of 13 other announced presidential candidates who don't even figure in these equations.

Let's say one of them — a Christian conservative like Mike Huckabee dedicated to preserving family values — emerges from the primaries with a pocket of strong supporters. Or one of the leading contenders starts strong in Iowa and New Hampshire, but stumbles on Super Tuesday. Or another gathers a bunch of delegates, then suspends his campaign, without releasing delegates, to play a kingmaker role at the convention. It is, to say the least, a fluid situation.

1952 was an interesting year for political conventions, especially because, for the first time, 70 million Americans were able to watch the proceedings on TV.

The Republican gathering in Chicago was a messy affair, pitting war hero Dwight Eisenhower against Ohio Sen. Robert Taft. Only after the Eisenhower forces unseated Taft delegates from Georgia, Louisiana and Texas was Eisenhower able to win nomination on the first ballot.

If the Republicans were messy, the Democrats were positively exhausting. Ten candidates were placed into nomination and negotiations over their eligibility, credentials, loyalty, and party platform positions stretched out into a six-day marathon, the longest convention in American history. In the end, the Democrats nominated Illinois favorite son Adlai Stevenson — on the third ballot.

Now imagine that scenario playing out in 2008 with hundreds of TV cameras scattered around the floor, and BlackBerries humming in every seat, and bloggers blogging, and funders funding, and pundits punding . . . oh, what journalistic joy we have to look forward to.

---

* When the Democratic National Committee later disqualified the Florida and Michigan delegations because they jumped their primary even further ahead of the February 5 cutoff date, the magic number needed for nomination became 2,026.

Later, the DNC Rules Committee would restore half those delegate votes, making the magic number 2,118. When the Democrats finally convened in August, with all parties agreeing on Obama's nomination, everyone got to vote since it no longer mattered.

Blog Along in Your Hymnals

May 04, 2007

THE DEMOCRATIC PRESIDENTIAL debate in South Carolina last week was of mild interest to me in that it was the first time all eight contenders appeared on stage together. Unfortunately, I found myself unable to get the MSNBC cable channel that sponsored the debate, so I sought out the insight of various Internet political commentators who were "live blogging" from the event. If trees were still involved in the dissemination of news, I would have to say this was a waste of good wood. In our now wired 24/7 Internet world, it turned out to be just a waste of time, which is why political blogging has become such a popular sport in America.

Campaigns & Elections, a bellwether source for campaign consultants and other political junkies, lists 419 sites in its directory of political blogs. *Technorati*, which has a more free form definition, puts the number of blogs about politics at 74,580. But even that estimate is probably low since there

April 27, 2007

1st Democratic debate with eight candidates

May 3, 2007

1st Republican debate with ten candidates

May 21, 2007

Bill Richardson enters race

are many more kitchen table commentaries, in all varieties of red state, blue state, liberal, conservative, libertarian and just plain snarky versions, hanging around in the MySpaces of the world.

As a matter of full disclosure, I too once had a blog. I started it in the early stages of the 2004 presidential campaign, but it soon became apparent I did not have the requisite number of opinions a day to keep up with the frenetic pace of my colleagues. So I settled back into my role as chief political correspondent of *The Week Behind,* taking full advantage of the seven day lull to collect my thoughts, do a little reporting, and present the reader with what mainstream media types still quaintly call "a story."

There are other websites on the Internet that do this, and do it well. *Slate* and *Salon* have excellent political reporters capable of crafting stories, and there is much excitement about the new *Politico.com,* started last January by *Washington Post* veterans John F. Harris and Jim VandeHei. In only a few months, they have corralled a staff of campaign trail veterans and given them the resources to roam the political landscape as only an Internet start-up can. When you add in all the efforts the mainstream media are making to post up their political stories on Internet sites in a timely fashion, political junkies have a wealth of coverage to access.

But it's probably a good idea to make the distinction right now between reporters who cover politics and bloggers who . . . what's the word I'm looking for here . . . blog politics.

I started my search for blog coverage of the debate at *Politico.com* where, sure enough, Ben Smith was live blogging from the event pressroom. It took me only a few minutes to realize watching a presidential debate in the presence of a live blogger is like sitting in the stands at a baseball game next to a loudmouth who won't shut up. Moment by moment, Smith fires off a comment on every jab and parry, scarfs up rapid-response notes for filler and, if there is nothing to write, offers up shout outs to his fellow reporters.

I switched over to the live blog MSNBC was doing in *The News Hole.* Now I wasn't sitting next to one drunk. I was sitting in a whole section of them blogging out one-liners about everyone and everything, including when's the best time to go out and have a cigarette.

I peeked in on the aptly named *Instapundit* where I discovered Glenn Reynolds, always ahead of his time, live blogging the live bloggers — telling us instantaneously the instantaneous comments he was reading on his favorite blogs. From Ann Althouse in Madison, to Jason writing for his MySpace page from a couch in Albuquerque, to Tigerhawk in Princeton, New Jersey, the debate was all things Mike Gravel, Reynolds reported.

In the new Democratic politics of the Internet, the *Daily Kos* has become blog central so I switched over to see what it was doing. What started four years ago as Markos Moulitsas Zuniga's personal campaign diary has blossomed into a major force on the left wing of the party. Through his website, Kos (his username) endorses candidates, raises money for their campaigns and, at the same time, publishes political "diaries" from a growing list of like-minded contributors.

On any given day, about 600,000 people tune into the *Daily Kos*. Bolstered by the local successes of his Democratic congressional endorsees in 2006, Kos held a convention of over 1,000 political bloggers in Las Vegas last year that attracted more than one potential 2008 Democratic contender.

The *Daily Kos* did not disappoint. Its home page was a virtual cacophony of blogging wit and wisdom. An "open thread" drew some 511 comments — and that was only during the first half of the debate. Here's a typical exchange in only a few minutes:

_ *Barack Doesn't sound nearly as smooth as I would have imagined. Gravel is an idiot. He was badmouthing the resolution that passed today. He said Congress should pass a law making it a crime to stay in Iraq. That is just STUPID!*
by manyoso

_ I second your Obama comment. Most people won't hear him in person, and on the radio/tv I've never found him too convincing. I'm glad that Gravel is there. He's another voice, and I think that's needed.

by skiddie

_ Barack . . . hasn't really been answering questions today.

by WhyWhat

_ Not Just Today . . .

by Grand Poobah

_As a constituent I agree.

by flatford39

_Gravel is right. It's too bad that he comes across as way too eccentric. He's useful, though. He makes the other candidates look more reasonable.

by metal prophet

_Gravel delivers the best Adm. Stockdale impersonation in years. "Who am I? Why am I here?" Indeed.

by Mogolori

_THANK YOU! I could not figure out who he reminded me of. LOL Bush Sucks. 'nuf said.

by Lobsters

_GRIDLOCK!!! n/t :) Obama-rama!

by boofdah

_Obama's performance thus far . . . can be described at shaky at best.

by Trix

_I agree. He's clearly been trying on the campaign trail in general not to go for the quick sound-bites, and that's good, because he does need to move beyond reliance, the dazzling smile, and the charisma. But in a debate you need to go for at least moderately quick answers.

by MissLaura

_Someone said he's not a good debater . . . in his Senatorial campaign, if I recall correctly. Not a good sign . . . so much seems to depend on debates in the general.
by cedubose
_Gravel rocks. Dodd too.
by Carolyn in Baltimore
_I suddenly love Gravel. He is amazing! "Scotty, get me the fuck outta here!" Jim Kirk
by steelman
_Gravel Is Terrible. He seriously thinks that Edwards/Obama/Clinton is going to preemptively nuke Iran? Get this guy off the stage, he's just wasting time attacking straw men.
George Dubya Bush Blows GWBblows Blog
by GWBblows

It is dangerous to paint all bloggers with the broad brush of self-indulgence. Mickey Kaus, who may have started it all with his *Kausfiles,* continues to be a timely, provocative voice in *Slate.* And I was a great admirer of Will Saletan's live blog from the floor of the Democratic convention in 2004 where he perfectly described a scene that I witnessed sitting only 100 yards away. But not every debate the Republicans or Democrats hold this season merits this kind of attention. In this new world where everyone can be a pundit, we must be careful of what we pretend to be because we are what we pretend to be, as Kurt Vonnegut famously stated. A world where everyone is a pundit is a world where punditry is the toilet paper of politics, useful only to wipe your own ass.

I suppose there is some odd value in all this. In the mash-up of insta-commentary, it's clear Mike Gravel has catapulted out of the obscurity of being a former Alaska Senator into being the next Dennis Kucinich. (And one enterprising blogger, midway through the debate, was already taking orders for T-shirts and bumper stickers saying "Gravel Rocks!")

It's going to be a long campaign and it's hard to see how all this idle prattle amounts to much more than preaching to the choir. MSNBC reports that the debate was viewed by two million people. Not all have their own blog so, obviously, somebody was listening.

Will Montana Pick The Next President?

June 01, 2007

THE LATEST MEMO coming out of the Clinton campaign suggests that Iowa is in danger of becoming irrelevant. "Thirteen of the last 14 major-party nominees have won Iowa, New Hampshire, or both," deputy campaign manager Mike Henry wrote his boss. "But I think this old system is about to collapse and it will happen this year because of the impact of primary elections that are being held on February 5."

Henry may have been ill-advised to release his thoughts to the media — and Sen. Clinton promptly promised to soldier on in the Hawkeye State despite her current third place standing — but there's more than a little truth in his reasoning.

On a nuts and bolts level, Henry predicts Sen. Clinton will have to spend $15 million and 70 days even to be competitive in Iowa, with no clear reward for winning.

June 13, 2007

Obama girl draws million viewers to you-tube

July 9, 2007

McCain fires staff, cuts back spending

July 15, 2007

Obama, Clinton set fundraising record, raising $58 million and $51 million, respectively, in first six months of 2007

In the best case, he says, "results are likely to be inconclusive on caucus night (first, second, and third place decided by a point or two) and they will provide little or no bounce for anyone . . . . Worst case scenario: this effort may bankrupt the campaign and provide little political advantage."

Henry's memo points up a dilemma for all the campaigns, Republican and Democratic: too little time in a compressed early primary schedule and — despite an abundance of money — too many places to spend it. Indeed, Adam Nagourney of the *New York Times* reports former New York Mayor Rudy Giuliani is considering doing just what Henry advises. I'd be surprised if, when push comes to shove, more candidates don't adopt his strategy.

The media attention on the Iowa caucuses is enormous so no candidate can actually skip Iowa. But the turnout at precinct caucuses is so slight (125,000 in the Democratic caucuses of 2004) and the stakes so meager (a proportional share of 45 delegates) it's hard to make a good cost-benefit argument for competing.

The best a candidate can hope is that he doesn't lose Iowa, a pitfall that Howard Dean demonstrated happens more often in the media aftermath than in the actual precinct voting. Show up, show well, and hope the single-digit showing for many of your competitors will convince them of the futility of continuing on. With eight Democrats and ten Republicans in the field, there's still going to be a gaggle of contenders coming out of the first turn — and running into uncharted territory ahead.

Only five days later, New Hampshire gives Iowa's losers a chance to resuscitate their campaigns in the nation's first primary, followed by a caucus in Nevada and two big primaries in South Carolina January 26 and Florida January 29 — and then the Big Kahuna: A Super Tuesday primary February 5 that will see 23 states go to the polls. These include New York, California, Illinois, Massachusetts, Alabama, Arkansas, Arizona, New Mexico, Georgia, Missouri, Connecticut, New Jersey, Tennessee and Colorado. As Henry notes in his memo, even a well-heeled candidate like Sen. Clinton could weather the early voting but find herself with only $10 million left to compete on this national stage. "This new focus forces us to rethink our overall strategy and assess where our time and money are best spent," Henry advises.

All of the campaigns, of course, hope to catch the "Big Mo" in the January contests and use it to "run the table" on Super Tuesday. Those are key phrases to watch for in the political coverage because the outcome of this race depends less on the votes accumulated by the candidates at that point than whether the media — whatever that is in this screwed-up election year — decides somebody has established momentum or, better yet, proven unstoppable in the big state showdown.

The chances a candidate in either party will have a majority of delegates after Super Tuesday are slim to none; and there aren't that many big states left — only Wisconsin on February 19; Ohio and Texas March 4; Pennsylvania April 22; and North Carolina and Indiana May 6.

So the search to build early momentum drives all the candidates to make an all-out effort in Iowa, but Henry has a word of caution for the momentum-ists as well. Before Iowans even arrive at the caucuses, absentee voters in Arizona, California, New Jersey, and Georgia may already be casting their ballots. In California, the state will mail out three million absentee ballots on January 7. If past elections are a guide, roughly a third of California voters will vote this way. Will they wait to see how the momentum is flowing — or mark it up and mail it in?

And what happens if nobody runs the table? Now, the scenario becomes even more intriguing. While candidates are off chasing votes in every little primary down the line, one part of the staff at the home office will be busy contacting party leaders and elected officials in both parties who attend the conventions as unpledged superdelegates. Another will start leafing through some pretty arcane party rules.

Look to the losers of the Florida and Michigan primaries to challenge the results. In defiance of both Republican and Democratic party rules, their state legislatures moved up the primary date ahead of February 5 knowing the penalty, according to party rules, is that neither delegation can be seated at the conventions so those votes won't be counted. If that rule is upheld, watch for Democrats to challenge other delegations because they don't have enough gay, lesbian and disabled delegates and/or because they didn't use their best efforts to install voting machines with paper trails (another party mandate.)

If there is no clear consensus winner on Super Tuesday, there are seven long months ahead until the conventions start. Start circling the firing squad, Democrats. It won't take long for the fissures among competing camps to appear. If you thought this campaign started early, it may not end until Montana metes out its 16 delegate slots June 3. Maybe one of them will be the vote that decides it all.

I was watching ABC News and they interviewed a woman in Iowa who was aghast that a candidate would skip the Iowa caucuses. "Why shouldn't they listen to us? We pay as much attention to the world as anyone else." I don't think it will be hard to find a similar sentiment among voters in Montana.

Sometimes it's good to be first. But sometimes it's great to be last.

The Dog Days of Politics

July 27, 2007

THEY CALL THIS time of year the dog days in journalism because it's so hot you can't get a dog to go out walking the streets. It's a time of scant news, editor vacations and now, it turns out, presidential debates staged for their entertainment value.

The *CNN/YouTube* Democratic debate Monday was up against some stiff competition — *Wife Swap, Age of Love* and *Are You Smarter Than a 5th Grader?* — but it managed to hold its own. Questions about global warming from a melting snowman, two Tennessee bumpkins wondering whether Al Gore's media attention hurt the candidates' feelings, and a singing question about taxes spiced up the evening — and gave all the candidates a chance to show they have a sense of humor.

Anderson Cooper moved the show along like a well-rehearsed Bert Parks, scattering different questions to only two or three different candidates (much to the consternation of Mike Gravel, who whined that he didn't get enough

July 23, 2007

CNN/YouTube Democratic debate

face time) and limiting responses to a level of brevity that must have made Joe Biden feel like he was answering in haiku.

All in all, the media response to the format was positive. Reporters even got a tidbit of news out of the debate in the exchange between Barack Obama and Hillary Clinton over whether they would be willing to meet with foreign leaders from Iran, North Korea, Cuba or Venezuela.

"The debate was certainly more lively than the usual candidate face-off," Adam Cohen wrote in the *New York Times*. "It was a bad night for news anchors and Washington bureau chiefs," added Steve Johnson in the Chicago *Tribune* because, as John Dickerson wrote in *Slate*, "The highly hyped experiment in user-generated content worked. In the privacy of their homes, people were at ease, and their videos reflected that. They sounded human. Had the same people been standing in the auditorium at the Citadel in Charleston, S.C., asking questions, they would have frozen up or tried to sound too polished."

The proof of the TV debate's success was in the pudding, or in television terms, the ratings: 2.8 million viewers (200,000 more than any previous debate this season) with impressive numbers in the coveted 18–34 age bracket. But even the novelty of the YouTube debate could not overcome the fundamental flaw in these things: too many candidates in too little time.

Hillary Clinton and John Edwards took flack after an earlier debate when off-camera mics caught them complaining about the gangbang approach to issues and promising to get their staffs together to work out a more closed-in arrangement. But Gail Collins, writing in the *Times* editorial page last Sunday, took up the cause and proposed her own television format: an American Idol series of debates where every week viewers vote off an obvious loser until only the strong survive.

I have my own suggestion, as long as we're in the silly season.

How about a March Madness debate tournament this August modeled after the NCAA basketball tournament. We divide the eight candidates into brackets, pit one against another based on national polls in quarterfinal and semi-final rounds, then let the last two candidates standing duke it out in Monday night primetime. We could call it the *ESPN/Note* debate.

Hillary Clinton (#1 seed) would face off against Mike Gravel (#8); Barack Obama (#2) could go against Dennis Kucinich (#7), John Edwards (#3) against Chris Dodd (#6), and Bill Richardson (#4) against Joe Biden (#5). In an hour-long format, each candidate would have at least one chance to talk at length about his or her positions: and we could throw in a lightning round or daily double question if that gets too tedious.

The cumulative effect of holding these debates on Friday, Saturday and Monday would give the spinmeisters ample time to force the candidates who move on to explain exactly what they meant in the earlier rounds, and oppositional research teams in each campaign time to zero in on the other guy's vulnerabilities.

It's fair, it's fun and, more important, in this silly season when no one cares about television or politics, it will fill a lot of airtime. Who knows? The Gonzaga U of politics might just turn out to be Mike Gravel. Wouldn't that be a kick in the pants!

In Defense of Inexperience

August 10, 2007

IF HOWARD WOLFSON has anything to say about it, you will come out of this August believing Barack Obama learned his foreign policy in kindergarten in Kansas and, after getting one right answer on a TRUE/FALSE quiz — should we invade Iraq? — failed all the rest.

Wolfson, the press secretary for Sen. Hillary Clinton, has a vested interest in proving Obama is "naive and inexperienced." He has taken Obama's answers to such questions as "should we talk with our enemies?" and "should we use nuclear bombs on Osama bin Laden? [answers: 1) yes, of course; and 2) no, of course not] to show the Illinois Senator is not as wise to the ways of the world as his own candidate.

In the debate in which the first question arose, Sen. Clinton was more nuanced in her response that she would meet with foreign leaders from Venezuela, Iran and North Korea only after lower level diplomats had set a clear agenda. But her response to Obama on the second was, in it's own way, just as naive.

The specific Obama quote that brought on Clinton's attack came in an Obama interview with the *Associated Press*. "I think it would be a profound mistake for us to use nuclear weapons in any circumstance," Obama said, adding, with a taint of regret, "involving civilians." Catching the oddity of his answer, he clarified it. "Let me scratch that," he said. "There's been no discussion of nuclear weapons. That's not on the table."

It wasn't, at least, until Sen. Clinton seized on the answer as another sign of her experience versus Obama's lack of same. "Presidents should be careful at all times in discussing the use and non-use of nuclear weapons," she said. "Presidents since the Cold War have used nuclear deterrence to keep the peace. And I don't believe that any president should make any blanket statements with respect to the use or non-use of nuclear weapons."

By leaving her nuclear guns "on the table," Clinton seems to believe she is demonstrating her foreign policy experience. Perhaps, given her range of experience, she can tell us how many times since the Cuban Missile Crisis in 1960, American presidents have threatened to use nuclear weapons. At a minimum, she ought to be able to tell us how many times her husband Bill Clinton threatened to use nukes during his eight years in office.

To score a few points for toughness, Sen. Clinton is, in effect, arguing against a half-century of effective arms control efforts that began with the recognition nuclear warfare will bring on mutually-assured destruction, and has led to significant new forms of global peacekeeping that have taken us back from the brinksmanship of the cold war. That, at least, is how I would phrase it were I writing for *Foreign Affairs*. But since all this bluster about who is more naive and inexperienced is taking place in the heat of a political campaign, let me put it this way: Babe, get a clue. Dropping a nuclear bomb on Pakistan is a bad idea. Just from a global warming perspective.

In the latest *New Republic*, Theodore Sorensen, John Fitzgerald Kennedy's speechwriter and confidante for 11 years, notes that the same charge of inexperience that is being leveled at Obama was once aimed at Kennedy. Like Obama, Kennedy, 40, was a first term Senator who entered the presidential race after an electrifying convention speech in 1956. His primary opponents in 1960 — Lyndon Johnson, Hubert Humphrey and Adlai Stevenson — all dismissed him as neither a powerhouse in Congress nor an experienced old foreign policy hand. At one campaign stop, Kennedy took up the challenge directly.

"Experience," he said, "is like taillights on a boat which illuminate where we have been when we should be focusing on where we should be going."

Indeed, if you look back at politics over the last 50 years, America has elected three "experienced" presidents — Lyndon Johnson, Richard Nixon and George H. W. Bush — and five "inexperienced" ones — John F. Kennedy, Jimmy Carter, Ronald Reagan, Bill Clinton and George W. Bush. How have we fared under each?

Johnson and Nixon can be credited with the worst foreign policy disaster of the 20th century. For all his experience, Johnson led America into the quagmire of Vietnam and Nixon not only extended the fiasco into neighboring countries but, fighting perceived enemies at home, broke into the Democratic party headquarters and got himself run out of office on a rail.

After a transitional two years under Gerald Ford, America chose the fresh face of Georgia Gov. Jimmy Carter to bring reform to Washington — and paid dearly for his inexperience when Iran seized American hostages in Tehran. When Carter's time was up, another inexperienced candidate named Ronald Reagan took charge. Reagan came into office almost pugnaciously "naive." But this time, standing outside the nexus of power, he articulated a fresh approach to dealing with the Soviet Union — how much fresher can you get than calling it an Evil Empire? — that brought a game-changing new perspective to the standoff of The Cold War.

The most successful of our experienced presidents was Reagan's successor, the first President Bush. He scored a triumphant victory over Saddam Hussein in Kuwait, shunned the idea of pushing forward into Iraq, and was rewarded by the American people with a resounding defeat at the polls after a single term.

Inexperience would not make a comeback on the political scene until 1992, when Bill Clinton brought it back in spades. The Clinton administration will be the most studied in American history because of all the contradictions inherent in how it worked out. But few candidates who were so singularly focused on domestic issues during a campaign — "It's the economy, stupid!" — have achieved so much in the foreign policy arena.

The last of the "inexperienced" presidents we have elected is our current President George W. Bush, who may also go down in history as our worst. The irony, of course, is that his most egregious foreign policy mistakes were not the result of his inexperience, but his reliance on his Vice President Dick Cheney and other old Washington hands whose experience in foreign affairs he acceded to.

Clearly, experience is overrated. From a statistical point of view alone, it appears we have a 60 percent chance of electing a good president when we choose someone who is not experienced, but only a 33 percent chance if we choose someone who is (and then we throw him out after one term.)

For an explanation why, let me give the last word to Sorensen on the similarities between Obama and Kennedy:

"Kennedy's speeches in early 1960, and even earlier, like Obama's in early 2007, were not notable for their five-point legislative plans. Rather, they focused on several common themes: hope, a determination to succeed despite the odds, dissatisfaction with the status quo, and confidence in the judgment of the American people."

"On civil rights, the Cuban Missile Crisis, the race to the moon, and other issues, President Kennedy succeeded by demonstrating the same courage, imagination, compassion, judgment, and ability to lead and unite a troubled country that he had shown during his presidential campaign. I believe Obama will do the same."

My Restless Legs Are Killing Us

August 24, 2007

SOMEWHERE IN THE middle of MSNBC's day long lead-up to the Democratic presidential debate in Chicago, somewhere between the never-ending ads for Flomax, Nexium, Lunesta, Ambien, Cialis, Cymbalta, Advocil, Enfacil, Expandex ad nauseum, it hit me.

How are these candidates going to fight the pernicious influence of the drug lobby in Washington when the drug companies are paying for this campaign? It's not just the bundled contributions they pour into the candidate coffers that influence campaigns; it's also the parade of TV drug advertising that fuels the cable news channels and underwrites the network news programs that cover them.

Not that I don't appreciate constant reminders that my bladder is leaking, my face is wrinkling, my prostate is growing, and my cholesterol is too high (or too low.) That's why, in fact, I see a doctor every year for a physical. But doctors will tell you they too are tired of patients coming

August 7, 2007

AFL-CIO Democratic debate in Chicago

August 11, 2007

Romney wins Iowa Republican straw poll

August 25, 2007

Democratic National Committee strips Florida of delegates, warns Michigan of same penalty for moving up primary dates

in to their office asking, as the TV ads instruct them, whether they might have less weary bones if they took this or that drug.

The pharmaceutical companies would have you believe this "direct to consumer" advertising is raising public awareness of health issues. They conveniently want you to forget that, prior to 1997, prescription drug advertising was banned on TV, just as is it in all other countries of the world except New Zealand. Sure, the ads come with disclaimers, but the disclaimers are so artfully integrated into the small type as to make doctors into footnotes to be consulted along with other reliable sources, like magazine ads in *Good Housekeeping* or websites they create and sponsor.

Lifting the ban on TV prescription drug advertising has been a boon to the drug companies. In the first year, spending in this category went from zero to $1.1 billion. It doubled the following year and continued to grow at an astounding pace until in 2006, it amounted to $5.3 billion, making drug advertising the fastest growing category on TV (except political ads.) So politicians who vow to stand up to the drug companies must actually take on not one but two of the most entrenched lobbyists in Washington: the drug companies and the media companies who thrive on their advertising dollars.

But it is a fight worth fighting, if only to rein in the kind of disease mongering that GlaxoSmithKline is conducting for a new drug called Requip designed to alleviate the suffering of Restless Legs Syndrome.

Clinically, Restless Legs Syndrome is defined as a "creepy-crawly" sensation in your legs that keeps you up at night. It is often misdiagnosed as insomnia. Drinking and smoking exacerbate the condition, and one of the potential drawbacks of the drug treatment, the ads alluringly suggest, is a heightened urge to gamble and have sex. [editor's note: how can I get me some?]

Little was known about Restless Legs Syndrome (RLS) until scientists at GlaxoSmithKline presented a paper on the disease to the American Academy of Neurology in 2003. By altering a drug called ropinirole used to treat Parkinson's Disease, they claimed to have found something that might alleviate some of the Restless Legs symptoms.

They submitted their findings to the Food and Drug Administration, including a telephone survey suggesting as many as 12 million Americans might be suffering from RLS, and helped underwrite a Restless Legs Foundation that turned this number into the oft-quoted factoid that one in ten Americans suffer from RLS.

The FDA reviewed the research (along with 54,000 other cases it handles every year) and in 2005 authorized GlaxoSmithKline to market Requip as a prescription drug remedy for Restless Legs. Over the next 12 months, Glaxo SmithKline spent $108 million advertising Requip on cable and broadcast TV. According to the disclaimer formula, the ads suggest I ask my doctor about Restless Legs Syndrome — so I did.

He is a highly respected internal medicine doctor with the Northwestern Medical Group in Chicago. In his 35 years of practice, he said, he has seen 5,000-7,000 patients and diagnosed RLS in, at most, 10 to 20 instances. So far he has prescribed Requip twice and, thankfully or not, neither patient reported elevated gambling or sexual activity.

One doctor's experience doesn't negate the raft of studies I'm sure GlaxoSmithKline amassed for FDA approval. But it does suggest that, in real life, the incidence of Restless Legs Syndrome is more like one out of 250 patients (.04 percent) than the one of out ten (10 percent) coming out of the company's research. But, of course, that could change the more GlaxoSmithKline advertises the disease — and its remedy.

"Disease mongering" is a term Steve Woloshin and Lisa M. Schwartz, two researchers at the Dartmouth Medical School and Veteran Affairs Outcomes Group, came up with after a study of the Requip marketing campaign. They describe it as "the effort by pharmaceutical companies to enlarge the market for a treatment by convincing people they are sick and need medical intervention.

"Typically, the disease is vague, with nonspecific symptoms spanning a broad spectrum of severity — from everyday experiences many people would not even call 'symptoms' to profound suffering," they wrote.

After GlaxoSmithKline introduced Requip to the market, the researchers found 33 articles in the media about the new drug, most of which closely followed the GlaxoSmithKline press releases. Invariably, reporters uncritically accepted the contention of widespread RLS suffering, relied on anecdotal stories from worst-case patients and glossed over possible long-term effects — never explored because FDA approval took only two years.

Through extensive advertising and PR campaigns, Woloshin and Schwartz concluded, drug companies expand the market for drugs like Requip "by narrowing the definition of health so normal experiences get labeled as pathologic" and including "earlier, milder, and presymptomatic forms."

Democratic candidates returning to Washington this September — they will return to Washington, won't they? — will have a clear opportunity to demonstrate their prowess in fighting the drug lobby, not just talk about it. They have, in fact, had that opportunity all year long as the House and Senate considered a re-authorization of the FDA through what is now called the drug safety bill.

Last January, buoyed by Democratic majorities in both the House and Senate, Rep. Henry Waxman (D-Ca) inserted a provision in the House version that would have forced drug companies to delay TV advertising for three years after FDA approval to allow more study of long-term effects.

But even this mild reform was stripped away last June in a house subcommittee where nine Democrats joined 14 Republicans to remove the restriction. As a result, neither the House nor Senate versions of the bill, now in a conference committee, contain limits on TV drug advertising, so that train has probably pulled out of the station.

But five of the eight Democratic candidates for president still have desks in Congress with microphones in front of them and cameras pointed at them. What better place to call out the Congressmen who caved in to the drug lobby or talk, in specifics and detail, about how the lobbying really works?

If Hillary Clinton is ready on day one to lead, why doesn't she call this "day one" and explain why, as leader of the New York Democratic delegation, she didn't raise a finger to stop Rep. Ed Towns (D-NY) and two other House Democrats from New York from nixing the Waxman proposal?

If Barack Obama wants to create a consensus for change, why doesn't he point the way by making it happen?

If Joe Biden or Chris Dodd or Dennis Kucinich aren't satisfied with the 90 seconds they get in debates to address the American people, why don't they use that bully pulpit, in this critical issue of health care, to show how they have made one iota of difference in this bill?

C-SPAN isn't YouTube and it's easy to dismiss the broadcast of congressional speeches as so much pablum. People said the same thing about Internet videos three years ago. But if we're going to fight the drug lobby, let's do it in Congress where the battle might do some good.

Otherwise, all this campaign posturing is so much blather. My attention will wander — and there's no telling what my restless legs will make me do.

Curb Our Dependence On Foreign Oil? Make a Wish!

September 14, 2007

YOU CAN'T RUN for public office these days without professing your commitment to curb our dependence on foreign oil.

Over the last five years, Congress has authorized more than $12 billion to subsidize exploration of new oil fields, wind power, solar power, nuclear power, "clean coal" and bio-fuels made from everything from corn and switch grass to wood chips and cow dung. But if you add up all the progress we've made developing these alternatives (and there has been progress) it still hasn't made a ding in the bumper of our gas hog of an economy.

Since President Bush announced his first national initiative to "curb our dependence on foreign oil" in 2002, the United States, in fact, has actually increased our oil consumption. Domestic production is down 650,000 barrels a day; domestic use is up 1,130,000 barrels a day; and we are making up the difference with a net increase of

1,860,000 more barrels of imported foreign oil a day than five years ago. Barring some unforeseen calamity, the natural growth of the American economy will leave the next president with the need to find and/or save at least a million more barrels of oil a day by the end of his first term in 2012 — just to keep foreign oil imports at the current level.

September 6, 2007

Fred Thompson enters race

September 12, 2007

Oil hits record $80 a barrel

All of the current candidates have a solution. Hillary Clinton wants to find "clean and homegrown" alternatives. Barack Obama wants to give the auto industry incentives to design more fuel-efficient cars. Mitt Romney wants to drill more wells in Alaska. Rudy Giuliani wants to build more nuclear energy plants. Dennis Kucinich wants to put more money into wind and solar power. But there's one point on which they all agree: we should curb our dependence on foreign oil.

So maybe it's time for a report card on what we can expect from all these alternatives. Let's look at them one at a time:

Solar and Wind Power

Environmental purists will tell you there is nothing more eco-friendly than solar and wind power, and they are probably right. The problem is harnessing that power. In the last five years, with heavy subsidies from both state and federal sources, wind-generated power stations in the United States have increased their output of electricity 250 percent and solar-generated electricity has grown 3.5 percent. These are, on the surface, impressive gains until one realizes this constitutes less than one percent of our energy consumption — and all of it goes into the electrical grid system.

Electricity remains an abundant resource in the United States. With the largest deposits of coal in the world, America generates just shy of 50 percent of our electricity from coal-fired power plants. Nineteen percent comes from nuclear plants; another 19 percent from natural gas, six percent from hydroelectric power dams and three percent from petroleum.

In the fight against global warming, wind and solar power are integral (although finding "clean" coal alternatives would have more impact.) But they have little to offer in the way of curbing our dependence on foreign oil.

Bio-fuels (ethanol from corn, switch grass and wood chips)

Ethanol is this year's fuel of the future (at least until the Iowa primary is over.) But what kind of ethanol? For the last five years, the federal government has poured billions into underwriting development of ethanol gas additives from corn. In addition to generous construction grants, producers receive a 51-cent subsidy for every gallon of ethanol they produce (which last year came to 4.9 billion gallons, or four percent of the U.S. motor gasoline production.)

Federal subsidies have grown the corn ethanol processing industry from 10 plants in 2000 to 110 today, with 76 more set to open in the next 12 months. These, in turn, will help meet Congress's stated goal of producing 7.5 billion gallons of ethanol by 2012 and President's Bush's announced (but unapproved) goal of producing 35 billion gallons by 2017.

There are, however, two flies in the ethanol ointment.

First, it takes 1.3 gallons of fossil fuel (mostly oil) to produce that one gallon of foreign oil replacement fluid.

Second, today's ethanol plants are soaking up so much of the available corn crop that the price of corn has risen from an average of $2.40 a bushel over the last two decades to $4 a bushel today, and the price increase is rippling through the U.S. economy in higher feedstock prices for farmers, more expensive meat prices for consumers, and attendant price hikes in other corn by-products affecting everything from corn syrup to cardboard packaging.

Ethanol advocates claim the gas additive leads to a 30 percent savings in oil consumption. But two university professors — David Pimentel of Cornell University and Tad Patzek of the University of California — set out two years ago to follow the ethanol production chain to determine the net energy gain or loss.

Taking into account the diesel fuel that goes into planting the corn, fertilizing the field, reaping the harvest, trucking the product to the plant, and operating the distilling process, they concluded corn-based ethanol requires 29 percent more fossil energy to create than it replaces. And other more nascent ethanol products fare worse. Switch grass requires 50 percent more fossil energy; wood biomass, 57 percent; and soybeans, 27 percent.

Only ethanol derived from sugar — used successfully in Brazil to fill 50 percent of its auto gasoline needs — has a positive energy balance yield. But Congress in its wisdom has put a 50-cent per pound tariff on imported sugar to protect American sugar farmers so we aren't even considering that.

The impact of America's rapid expansion of ethanol production, moreover, is also vastly over-rated. When the billions of gallons annually are measured like oil in millions of barrels a day, the projected domestic ethanol production in 2012 will fill less than 0.5 percent of America's oil needs.

Hybrids and Hydrogen

Automobiles, airplanes and other transportation vehicles account for roughly two-thirds of our domestic oil consumption. So it goes to figure that more fuel-efficient cars will lead to lower gasoline consumption. This is the premise behind the hybrid automobiles that seamlessly shift between gas engines and rechargeable batteries to yield 50-60 miles per gallon versus the current American automobile average of 27.5.

Hybrids came into the American market in 1999 with the introduction of the Honda Insight, followed eight months later by the first Toyota Prius. Despite a promised 70 mpg, neither sold particularly well. They were pricey compared to other standard models; and with gas selling at $1.29 a gallon, fuel-economy was not on anyone's mind.

In 2003, about the same time gas prices were jumping up over $3.00, Toyota redesigned the Prius and launched it with a PR campaign that made it an eco-friendly status symbol in Hollywood. It didn't hurt that Congress the next year gave hybrid car buyers a tax deduction worth $600. When Congress turned that deduction into a tax credit worth up to $3,100 in 2006, sales of hybrid cars took off.

This year, Toyota and Honda will sell nearly 250,000 hybrid cars; and every major auto manufacturer is jumping on the bandwagon with hybrid models of trucks, SUV's and even light trucks. By 2015, Edmunds.com estimates that sales of new hybrids will reach 1.7 million a year.

Unfortunately, that is still only 11 percent of the new vehicles made in America every year; and, as efficient as hybrids are, they will be sharing the road with 250 million older legacy cars, trucks, semi-trailers and other vehicles tethered to the old gas-guzzling technology.

In Detroit, forward-thinking auto designers are looking beyond gas and electric-powered cars to vehicles that operate entirely on hydrogen. In his 2003 state of the union speech, President Bush dedicated $1.7 billion toward research aimed at developing a practical hydrogen car by the year 2020.

Hydrogen-powered cars are an alluring proposition. Not only do they replace gasoline as a power source but the tailpipe emissions after combustion produce no greenhouse gases to increase global warming. The problem here is that hydrogen is an energy carrier not an energy source. The power behind hydrogen cars must be created elsewhere (current experimental models use six sources, half of which require fossil fuels.) To become a viable means of transportation, someone will also have to invent a way to produce, store, transport and distribute hydrogen to all the vehicles on the road.

Multiple technical and financial breakthroughs will be needed before hydrogen cars become practical. The most optimistic guess is that we will have that technology in hand by 2030, but it won't be until 2050 that we will have a nationwide system of fuel stations in place to service these vehicles.

Will that curb our dependence on foreign oil?

Exploration vs. Conservation

There is a legitimate argument to be made that if the conservationists would take the clamps off the drilling in the Artic National Wildlife Refuge in Alaska, we might add another 600,000 to 1.6 million barrels of oil a day to our domestic production capacity. Before that can happen, however, we will need to find it and build a pipeline or other supply route to get it out.

In a best case scenario, if Congress acted tomorrow to allow that drilling, the first trickle of oil from the region wouldn't reach the United States until 2017 and it wouldn't be until the year 2029 that production would reach full capacity, most likely around 900,000 barrels a day.

We also know there are pockets of oil still untapped in the deep waters of the Gulf of Mexico and closer in along the Florida coast (where conservationists have so far blocked development). Congress authorized $2.8 billion in 2005 in tax incentives to oil companies to spur that exploration (not that anyone's holding a tag day for them.) But record profits from current operations, complex technical issues reaching the oil, and second thoughts after the oil rig damage from Hurricane Katrina have combined to slow development.

Yet another prospect for finding new oil on this continent lies in northern Canada where various oil company consortiums are developing expensive, but promising new technologies to extract oil from tar sands. The Canadian National Energy Board recently upped its estimate of the potential yield to as much as 3 million barrels a day by 2015, in part because higher oil prices are making the expense more affordable, and planning is well underway for a pipeline to take this oil directly through Canada to the Chicago refineries.

Closer to home, the Bush administration won congressional approval in the 2005 energy bill to conduct an environmental impact study on using similar methods to extract oil from shale deposits in a Rocky Mountains region known as the Green River Formation.

The Green River runs through federal lands at the corner of Utah, Colorado and Wyoming. A thousand feet below the surface, the U.S. Energy Department estimates, as much as two trillion barrels of oil lies trapped in the shale — eight times the oil reserves of Saudi Arabia. Mining that shale, processing the rock to extract the oil and disposing of the remnants would create a mountain of refuse five times higher than Aspen. But, hey, with the right contouring, wouldn't that be a great ski hill?

Leaving aside the pesky fact that the exploration area cuts through both the Flaming Gorge and Dinosaur National Wildlife areas, the logistics of extracting this shale oil are daunting. Not only would we have to dig down 1,000 feet to reach the shale layer, but we would need to create a whole new industry devoted to shale oil processing in

Wyoming. To Dick Cheney, who championed this lost cause, that's an opportunity. To the rest of us, it's a nightmare.

The flipside of finding new oil is using less of it. The surest path to assuring less oil consumption is a federal mandate raising fuel efficiency standards for cars and small trucks. Congress first tried this in 1975 in response to the Arab oil boycott. Inside of ten years, American automobiles went from averaging 12 miles a gallon to 24 miles a gallon. The rising federal standard peaked in 1987 at 27.5 miles per gallon. As oil prices dropped, so did the need to conserve and that is where it remains today.

This fall, Congress will again consider raising the standard. A consensus is developing around a plan by Democratic candidates Barack Obama and Joe Biden (among others) to increase the fuel efficiency standard by four percent a year until it reaches 35 miles a gallon by the year 2020. When fully implemented, the higher standard will save 1.3 million barrels of oil a day, more than can be expected from Alaskan oil drilling, ethanol processing, hydrogen cars, solar or wind power. But is it enough?

The Reality

The reality is nothing underway or proposed will cut our dependence on foreign oil — it will only slow its growth.

Every day America uses 21 million barrels of oil, some 12.4 million of which comes from foreign sources. Former Energy Secretary James Schlesinger, now an oil company executive with the Mitre Corporation, says the idea of America achieving oil independence is a "flaw of perception" perpetrated by politicians to demonstrate they won't be held hostage by hostile forces in the Middle East.

But the Middle East is where 70 percent of the world's known oil reserves lie and the global price of energy is set. Maybe it's time to embrace our friends in the region instead of fearing them — while we still have a few left.

The irony of the last five years is that while Americans floundered about looking for alternatives to oil, Saudi Arabia has been quietly spending $25 billion to raise its oil output. It has retro-fitted drilling operations in the mammoth Gahwar oil fields and established mega-projects offshore in the Arabian Gulf and in the Rub al-Khali desert that, over the next five years, will pump out as much as 4 million more barrels of oil a day.

If our venture into Iraq doesn't lead to Sunni-Shia strife that spills out through the region, that should stabilize world oil supplies long enough to allow our alternative energy programs in the United States to get a foothold.

But if you're looking for the one sure way to curb our dependence on foreign oil, make Saudi Arabia our 51st state.

---

* Unless otherwise noted, figures used in this article are derived from reports by the Energy Information Agency of the U.S. Energy Department.

Let's Hear It For The Underdog

November 2, 2007

I TAKE A PERVERSE pleasure in watching the 2008 Republican candidates vie to take up the banner George Bush has left them after eight years in office. It's a little like watching people volunteer to lead a suicide squad.

Eight contenders have emerged for the honor, but the mainstream media are treating them like also-rans. The more meaty dish of whether Hillary, Barack or John Edwards will outwit the others to lead the Democrats back to the White House is, frankly, far more tasty.

To be sure, the Republican candidate who grabs the nomination has a long uphill trek ahead. Not only will he have to prove he is more popular than the current president — whose approval ratings are hovering around 30 percent — but also able to win over 21 percent of the remaining electorate to the notion that he can lead America in a new direction. Sisyphus had an easier task.

Just last week, a *Los Angeles Times/ Bloomberg* poll showed a majority of Americans now believe the economy is on the wrong track. That is the highest no-confidence vote in five years. Sixty-five percent say they have not benefited from the Bush tax cuts, and 60 percent say they favor repeal of some tax cuts to fund one of the Democratic proposals for more federal health care. Add in the discontent over Iraq and general Bush fatigue, and it's shaping up to be one tough year to be a Republican.

What I like about the Republican side of the race is that, unlike the Democrats who have to decide who best represents the party, the Republicans have to decide what the hell the party stands for. Without Karl Rove around to mediate the conflicting interests, it's anyone's guess.

Front-running Rudy Giuliani epitomizes the problem. The former New York mayor won his first (and only) elective office by being an un-Republican: a tough-talking federal prosecutor, he wooed the normally Democratic voters of New York city with pronouncements that were strongly pro-choice on abortion, lenient on gay marriage and vociferous on the need for gun control laws.

His tenure in office was marked by a crackdown on petty crime and austere fiscal measures, both trademarks of Republicanism, but also light-hearted appearances in drag at social events and a messy divorce and remarriage, none of which fall into the category of Republican family values.

His presidential candidacy is propelled by his response as "America's Mayor" to the 9/11 attack on the World Trade Center. But aside from his determination to fight the war against terrorism on foreign shores, he has come up notably short on original ideas for how to win it in Iraq, Afghanistan, Iran or wherever else it is sure to break out.

Far more suited to the Republican mantle is Mitt Romney, the management consultant turned Republican governor of Massachusetts (another Democratic stronghold). His family values credentials are straight out of a Norman Rockwell painting — if Rockwell had painted Mormons — and his trust in sound business practices to solve America's social problems would make Calvin Coolidge proud.

Like Giuliani, he hails from what used to be called the Eastern Establishment (or Rockefeller) wing of the party, which has been a waning force since the ascension of Barry Goldwater in 1964; and he is proving to be more of a flip-flopper than John Kerry, or what you'd call a Republican John Kerry without the war record.

The power base of the Republican Party lies in the South, the western plains and a dozen or so key Midwestern states. They are sparsely represented in the race this year. Mike Huckabee, the former Arkansas governor and Baptist preacher, is a likeable enough candidate in this mode. If his organization were stronger, he might have garnered more support from the religious right and been right in the thick of things. Fear that Huckabee didn't have a widespread base drove the Christian conservatives to look for an alternative, settling on "Law & Order" actor Fred Thompson.

The hope was that Thompson could be another Ronald Reagan. He is not. He shares Reagan's ability to deliver a good conservative line, but only when it is written out for him.

Reagan honed his message wandering in the desert of conservatism for two decades before he brought his crusade to Washington. Thompson, for all practical purposes, lives there. The primaries for Thompson are an out-of-town tryout tour of backwater stages, but his act doesn't improve from one to another. As down home as he tries to be, he leaves the locals with the notion he would rather be somewhere else.

John McCain and Ron Paul also hail from the Goldwater wing of the party—McCain as Goldwater's successor in the Senate from Arizona, Paul by virtue of his previous presidential run as the Libertarian party candidate. Strangely, neither seems to be benefiting from it.

Okay, so Paul was a long shot to begin with and his call for an immediate withdrawal from Iraq is heresy to the current party leaders. But what, pray tell, is wrong with John McCain?

It was not that long ago that McCain himself was the frontrunner in the race. He'd mended fences with the president, reached out to Jerry Falwell with an olive branch of peace and briefly led the Republican fundraising sweepstakes.

A top-heavy campaign staff did little to capitalize on that lead (and blew through most of the money) so earlier this year McCain trimmed his sails and reverted to the "one truthful man" campaign tactics that worked so well for him in 2000. And that is what makes him so appealing.

McCain is dogged by the fact that the religious right has not embraced his campaign. James C. Dobson, the founder of Focus on the Family, was largely credited with delivering four million evangelicals to Rove in 2004, thus cementing President Bush's re-election. Primed to do the same in 2008, he early on rejected McCain as not in tune with his movement.

McCain, however, is apparently not the only candidate who hasn't met Dobson's high standards. Dobson has gone on to reject Giuliani for his liberal social views, Romney for his Mormonism and Thompson for his lack of substance. Of late, Dobson, 71, has taken to talking about a third party as the only way to carry on his crusade.

It's unclear who will follow Dobson out of the party. The religious right is a fractured political force this year. In a Sunday *New York Times* magazine piece this week, David Kirkpatrick points out that Dobson's influence is waning. Younger mega-church leaders like Rick Warren in California and Bill Hybels in suburban Chicago have a broader, less ideological approach to carrying out God's mission. For the first time in a decade, toeing the religious right's line on social issues may not be the litmus test of Republicanism.

If that proves the case, McCain has as strong a claim on Republican values as any of the other candidates. Perhaps more. He's been a clear advocate of fiscal responsibility in federal spending — and more, an effective legislator in making government more efficient.

He spearheaded campaign finance reform and, when his McCain-Feingold reforms came under attack, wasn't afraid to admit the errors while at the same time explaining how compromise with resistant senators brought them about.

If Hillary Clinton wins the Democratic nomination because of her seven years experience in the Senate, McCain can trump her on a dozen fronts with his 21, most of it spent working both sides of the aisle to make the federal government work better.

Of all the Republican candidates, he is the only one who has taken a principled stand on Iraq. He favored toppling Saddam Hussein; he criticized Bush for the inept way he did it; he said the United States needed to commit more troops to the cause; and when Bush did — in the form of Gen. David Petraeus's "surge" — he staked his candidacy on its success.

Right or wrong, you know where John McCain stands — and stood over the last five years of the Iraq War.

He is also, it bears repeating, a war hero: the premise behind the Democrat's choice of John Kerry in 2004. After being shot down as a Navy pilot in Vietnam, McCain stoically suffered five years of excruciating torture as a North Vietnamese prisoner-of-war.

While Mitt Romney (who skipped that war on a deferment) waffled this month on whether waterboarding actually constitutes torture, McCain had no such reservations. Been there, done that. It's torture — and unacceptable in a freedom-loving nation such as ours.

McCain has a way to go to work himself back into Republican contention. The disarray in his campaign organization forced him to all but forego the Iowa caucuses. But a better than expected showing in New Hampshire — which he won in 2000 over a Texas candidate named George Bush — could jump start his campaign. That makes him viable in South Carolina, where the military vote matters, and with a good showing, peaking just in time for Super Tuesday.

I don't suppose the fate of John McCain will garner much attention among political reporters now focused on whether Hillary can close out the Democratic contest on Super Tuesday. But let me repeat, one if not both parties are headed to a convention where none of the contenders has the nomination sewn up.

In the Republican case, the convention will have to decide not only who will stand to defend the principles of the party, but what those principles are. They could do a lot worse than to make John McCain that man.

The Campaign No One Is Watching

November 9, 2007

I'VE OFTEN WONDERED how politicians can waste so much money running for office. Now the advent of political videos on YouTube has given me new insight into the answer.

To date, the Republican and Democratic candidates for president have produced a combined 2,434 Internet videos on YouTube — and it is still 60 days before the first voters go to the polls.

I'd like to say I watched them so you don't have to, but even I'm not that much of a political masochist. The best I can do is count them. So here's the leaderboard in Internet videos:

Republicans:
Mitt Romney 436
Rudy Giuliani 226
Tom Tancredo 148

November 12, 2007

Iowa Jefferson-Jackson Day Dinner

December 10, 2007

New York Times/ CBS Poll

Republicans:
Giuliani 22%
Huckabee 21%
Romney 16%
McCain 7%

Democrats:
Clinton 44%
Obama 27%
Edwards 11%

December 16, 2007

Ron Paul collects $6 million in single day of Internet fundraising.

Mike Huckabee 92
John McCain 86
Ron Paul 62
Fred Thompson 34
Duncan Hunter 20

Democrats:
Barack Obama 247
John Edwards 230
Chris Dodd 205
Joe Biden 191
Bill Richardson 183
Dennis Kucinich 112
Hillary Clinton 88
Mike Gravel 74

Only nine months ago, Internet videos were viewed as the hot new commodity in politics. Barack Obama announced his candidacy in a video release. Hillary Clinton launched hers with a series of fireside chats dubbed "Conversations." Candidates rushed to set up YouTube accounts, MySpace friend networks, and an attendant staff of videographers, editors and compressionists to follow their every move and post up snippets of their campaign appearances.

But the evidence so far is that nobody is watching. Except for the occasional anchor spot — a slick commercial sure to make its way onto broadcast television in the early primary states — most videos are being seen by only a couple thousand viewers. Over a two month period, a viewership of less than 1,000 people is often the norm — and most of those are political junkies, usually rabid fans.

Mitt Romney, for instance, leads the pack with 436 posted videos on YouTube, some 219 of which are repeated on MySpace TV. His MySpace video plugs have been seen 72,000 times, which translates to an average audience of 329 people for every video post.

You want to know how flawed this Internet video strategy is? I went to the YouTube page for political videos called "You Choose" last Sunday and found, under the Republican column, that the buttons linking to each candidate's introduction were misdirecting viewers to the next candidate's site. It was a minor programming glitch, easily corrected. But it wasn't fixed for three days. Did anyone complain? Not hardly. Because no one is watching.

There have been a few notable exceptions, but they are usually in a humorous vein. The original "Obama Girl" and the inspired mash-up of an Apple "1984" commercial with Clinton footage have each been seen four million times. But Clinton's own highest-rated spot — "I Need Your Advice" — has garnered only 633,000 views. And what advice was she seeking? She was asking people to suggest a campaign theme song and promising she would not attempt to sing it.

Obama's initial foray onto YouTube to announce his candidacy nine months ago remains his highest-rated self-produced video with 398,000 views. But a quick clip of his appearance in a Halloween spoof on Saturday Night Live five days ago already has been seen 580,000 times and is likely to soar past a million.

The Internet has once again confounded our politicians, just as it has the rest of us. They know they must have a presence there, but they don't know what it should be. That's why Barack Obama hired Joe Rospars, the founder of Blue States Digital, to run his Internet operation. That's why John Edwards has Joe Trippi, the Internet guru behind Howard Dean's campaign, as his chief political advisor. That's why Tom Tancredo, a little known Colorado Congressman running on the single issue of building a fence around Mexico to stop illegal immigrants, has found a way to say the same thing in 184 different videos, as if anyone cares.

What are they getting for their Internet video efforts? They don't know and neither do the rest of us. What we've learned from the YouTube election so far is that the cutting edge of technology is a dangerous place for a candidate to be. (Just ask Howard Dean.) The cache that attaches to a candidate who rides the latest technological wave impresses some, but leaves the rest of the country — older, stodgier, and more likely to vote — in its wake.

Judging from the campaign so far, the driving force behind the 2008 race are the political polls — and, once again, how mainstream media like the *New York Times* and *Washington Post* interpret them.

The pundits of the blogosphere — Matt Drudge, *The DailyKos*, Josh Marshall, Taegan Goddard and others — have influence precisely because they are read by the mainstream media; and now that mainstream reporters themselves are shifting over to sites like *Politico.com* or writing more for the online extensions of their own publications, traditional campaign reporting is more important than ever. The game this year is managing media expectations and perceptions.

Our next president will come out of a process that is tried and true. Iowa voters will leave the comfort of their homes on a cold night in January to stand in a local gymnasium or VFW hall and say who they like, and why. New Hampshire voters will cast ballots in their first-in-the-nation primary and the winner in either party is not likely get more than 80,000 votes. The rest of us will march along to the drumbeat of succeeding primaries led by a fife and drum corps of political reporters who have trudged from one tarmac to another accumulating little insights on the candidates. How they report these will shape a race that most of us will just watch on TV.

Every day, every week, someone will call us on the telephone to ask who we now favor, and the news media will report him or her to be the frontrunner, regardless of how many delegates they have collected. But none of us, I guarantee you, will say I like Candidate X because he had a really great video on YouTube.

Skipping Iowa

December 27, 2007

SORRY BOYS, I'M not coming out. Not yet. Not until you all cool your jets and settle in for the long slog. You've already booked every motel room inside of 100 miles of Des Moines, but I'm telling you now, on the eve of the first presidential voting, Iowa is a sucker's bet.

I'm going to watch this mythical end to your mythical media campaign on television like most Americans, switching back and forth between your on-scene coverage and the Orange Bowl, where Virginia Tech and Kansas will be playing the same night in sunnier climes. I'll tune in long enough to hear who "won" Iowa, but I won't place much credence in the reports. Here's why:

When Iowa goes to the polls next Thursday, there will be no polls. Instead, there will be 3,562 American Legion halls, school gymnasiums and local taverns that, at 6:30 PM, will turn into gathering points for loyal Republicans and Democrats in every precinct in Iowa to meet and kick off the presidential season.

January 3, 2008

Iowa caucuses (Obama, Huckabee)

January 4

Biden drops out
Dodd drops out

January 5

Wyoming Republican caucuses (Romney)

Some will have several hundred people in attendance; others as few as a couple dozen. The legal purpose of these precinct caucuses is to select some 14,000 delegates to attend county conventions in March that, by June, will narrow themselves into delegates to a state party convention where Iowa's 40 Republican and 57 Democratic delegates will ultimately be named to attend their national conventions.

What draws the major presidential contenders and the national media to Iowa every four years is the fact that somewhere in the middle of these proceedings, attendees are asked to show their preference for a presidential candidate.

Republicans do this by putting names in a hat (not binding on county convention delegates selected); Democrats by dividing themselves into different corners of the room based on their candidate preference. If any one corner has less than 15 percent of the total caucus attendees, that group must disband and align with another. It's an arcane, outdated process, but leads to a lot of grassroots discussion about who best represents Iowa.

At the end of the night, each caucus calls its results in to state party officials.

State party officials then round off the number of county delegate slots assigned to each contender (based on a weighted measure of the voting) and use a mathematical algorithm to simplify the totals into "state delegate equivalents" that are released to the media on election night to show who "won."

As imprecise and indecipherable as the process is — even in a good year, less than 10 percent of Iowa's eligible voters participate — winning Iowa has somehow become ingrained in the American political psyche as the first critical step on the road to the presidency.

But this may be the year that theory collapses under the weight of its own popularity, especially if the race is so close it exposes the inherent flaws in the system.

The attention lavished on Iowa over the last nine months has been an order of magnitude greater than in any other previous campaign. John Edwards has spent 187 days there; Barack Obama has spent 119; Mitt Romney, 113; Mike Huckabee, 111; and Hillary Clinton, 105. Connecticut Sen. Chris Dodd, a long shot to begin with, moved his family to Des Moines and enrolled his kid in the public schools.

There are estimates all the candidates will spend a combined $50 million on radio, TV and junk mail advertising this year (roughly five times 2004's record-setting pace.) Even after all that attention, 40 percent of Iowa's voters say they are still undecided six days before the voting.

Whatever the candidates wind up spending on Iowa, the media outlets covering the race will probably spend more. The largest caucus convening in Iowa next Thursday will be at the Des Moines Convention Center where some 2,500 reporters are expected to draw media credentials.

If the candidates have spent more time in Iowa than ever, so have the reporters covering them. Not one or two old veterans with big-pocket sponsors fulfilling the promise of "all the news that's fit to print." Gaggles of them — often outnumbering citizens at candidate events — reporters, stringers, citizen journalists and others feeding the cable channels, newspapers, blogs and entertainment shows.

Running for president is the new national sport. You don't have to do it because you can watch others do it on TV and the Internet (and post your opinion as a "comment" on the story you are reading.) The political campaign now has its own cable channels (CNN, MSNBC and Fox), websites (Drudge, Politico, Real Clear Politics), blogs (too many to name) and even its own XM/ Sirius outlet (The Political Channel). They've all been hard at it covering the race for almost a year. All they need now is for someone to vote.

Those of us who do not live in Iowa, New Hampshire or South Carolina probably haven't seen a single paid political commercial by any of the candidates. Yet we feel like we've seen them all on the nightly news, Sunday talk shows and cable news stations. We've read all the candidate profiles on the front page of the *New York Times*; seen the YouTube clips of their gaffs; surfed the blog reports on their staff shake-ups; and, most insidiously, been subjected to opinion poll on top of opinion poll — as many as 40 in a single month — telling us who is surging, sinking, and sunk.

So Iowa going to the polls is a welcome relief from all the bluster, or a reminder that, in a race where 17 candidates are still lined up at the starting gate, 15 of them will lose.

It is the media's craving for someone to win that stokes this madness. My favorite moment in the campaign so far came in early December when an NBC reporter accompanying Obama on his tour bus asked, "Now that the campaign is coming to an end, do you feel you've gotten your message across?" Obama looked at him with a suppressed smile. Coming to an end? This is still the pre-season, dude. Get a clue.

It will be interesting to see how the TV networks report from Iowa on election night. Many of the caucuses will still be going when they first break into their regularly scheduled programming. As Roger Simon noted in *Politico.com*, they will hang these early returns on the most dubious of concepts — "entrance polls" conducted at 40 Republican and 40 Democratic caucus sites semi-scientifically selected by the same people who predicted Al Gore would be president and misled John Kerry into thinking he would.

As attendees walk into the caucus, they will be asked not only their candidate preference but 16 questions on issues, attitudes, impressions and outlook. In a close contest, the candidate preferences will be withheld. But there should still be plenty of grist for the mill of pundits and commentators that will grind away over the course of the night showing off the new sets, graphics, websites and political teams each network will be fielding this season.

Sometime around the third quarter of the Virginia Tech-Kansas game, there should be enough precincts reporting for the networks to put percentage totals up on the scoreboard next to candidate names. Maybe, in the fourth quarter, even a check mark for the "winner" will appear.

Don't expect any actual vote totals to go up on the leader board. Iowans don't tally votes. They meet and discuss the issues at hand. They test the candidates with tough questions and talk among themselves about the answers. That was once what made Iowa so appealing to reporters trying to get a handle on the campaign ahead. Now it may be Iowa's downfall.

Too many people have invested too much time in Iowa not to come away with a winner.

But whoever that winner is, remember this: they probably won't win more than 16 delegates and the runner up could well wind up with 15 — out of the 4,417 Democrats and

2,516 Republicans who will take seats at the national conventions next fall.

There's plenty of racing ahead. So pack up your laptops, bid a fond farewell to the butter cow at the Iowa state fair and get your ass up to New Hampshire. I'll be waiting.

See you on the tarmac.

Midnight at The Wayfarer

January 11, 2008

BEDFORD, NEW HAMPSHIRE — It's midnight at The Wayfarer, the witching hour and the ghost of politics past hangs in the air.

Hunter Thompson once described this resort hotel on the campaign trail as "The Valley Forge of presidential politics." But it seems now to have fallen on hard times. Space heaters are strategically placed around the hallways to bolster a central heating system run amok. A sign on the public washroom directs guests down the hall because this one is out of order. More alarming, the rapid-fire spin and bluster I expected to find in the bar after the *ABC Facebook* doubleheader debate Saturday night — three days before the New Hampshire primary — is drowned out by the whoops and pings of a video golf game. The famous Wayfarer Inn lounge has become a sports bar.

Oh sure, there are a few old hands still hanging around. *Time*'s Joe Klein and *Washington Post* columnist E. J. Dionne hold down the end of the bar; and a couple correspondents

January 8

New Hampshire primary (Clinton, McCain)

January 10

Richardson drops out

and producers from CBS, the last network to still headquarter there, are scattered around the tables. Klein regales two fresh-faced admirers with stories of primaries gone by. But the mystique is gone — and so are the people.

This year, the action has shifted downtown to The Radisson, a glitzy high-rise hotel with a convention center attached. ABC is there, running three shows and an extensive web operation out of a converted exhibit hall. Fox News has another. NBC and MSNBS broadcast from an old armory accessible through a closed-in causeway. CNN has booked 60 rooms. And there's a "Talker's Row" up on the second floor where a couple dozen talk radio hosts from around the country gab away day and night.

Where the media gather, so do the politicians. Or the handlers, at least, whose job is to cultivate friendships and massage the news as it makes its way to the airwaves — "lubricate the facts," as it was once described to me.

For that, the Radisson has J.D.'s Tavern, a poor substitute for the old Wayfarer lounge but blessed by the fact that it is located in the Grand Central Station of this year's race.

Not that proximity is as important as it used to be. Everyone has Black-

Berries. The daily campaign schedules are online. And the people who need to know aren't just reporters but literally thousands of drivers, advancemen, embeds, stagehands, bloggers and other aptly-named facilitators who are camped out in local motels. [Editor note: *The Week Behind* worked out of the Red Roof Inn on Spit Brook Road.]

The candidates themselves are spread out across the state. Barack Obama and John Edwards are at the Radisson in Nashua. Mitt Romney is in Portsmouth. Hillary Clinton has three headquarter hotels in Manchester. And John McCain — well, he just hangs by his thumbs from the nearest tree at the end of every day so he can rise from the dead again in the morning.

What happened to The Wayfarer may be what is happening in politics this year. After 25 years in the hands of the caring Dunfey brothers, The Wayfarer was sold off to a succession of hotel chains, all promising to modernize it. One found the land so valuable it sold off the front entrance for a Macy's shopping center. Then the state lopped off the back to build a new Interstate tollway. All the reporters could see The Wayfarer was going downhill, but no one wanted to say anything. So they quietly found other accommodations. Finally, it fell into the hands of a real estate investment group that made it a Quality Inn franchise. But re-branding The Wayfarer as a Quality Inn was like putting lipstick on a pig. Change had been needed for a long time. Now it was obvious.

The Second Coming of Barack

Barack Obama came out of Iowa into the New Hampshire primary with more good press than Jesus ever got, even on Palm Sunday. Months of debate over whether change or experience would drive the 2008 campaign has been resolved decisively in favor of change, and Obama is its new Messiah.

The Iowa caucuses were hailed as a new day in American politics. A freshman senator from Illinois, a black man preaching the politics of hope, had bested the fabled Clinton political machine in a Midwestern state with a 98 percent white population. To put a punctuation mark on the victory, Obama used his election night podium to deliver a stirring call to arms for Americans that was instantly compared to the best of Martin Luther King.

"There is no getting around it, this man who emerged triumphant from the Iowa caucuses is something unusual in American politics," Michael Powell wrote in the *New York Times*. "He has that close-cropped hair and the high-school-smooth face with that deep saxophone of a voice. His borrowings, rhetorical and intellectual, are dizzying. One minute he recalls the Rev. Dr. Martin Luther King Jr. in his pacing and aching, staccato repetitions. The next minute he is updating John F. Kennedy with his 'Ask not what America can do for you' riff on idealism and hope."

The underlying truth of Obama's Iowa victory is that it was based on a superior field organization. Steve Hildebrand, Obama's deputy campaign manager, began building it more than a year before the caucuses, recruiting the same local party activists he successfully managed for John Kerry in 2004 and harnessing their foot power to a central database that identified potential caucus supporters — and the arguments that would sway them to Obama.

Obama's charisma brought out thousands of other volunteers, many from out-of-state. Wary of how Howard Dean turned his "perfect storm" of student volunteers into a perfect disaster, the Obama campaign put the volunteers through extensive training sessions to teach them how not to come across as carpetbaggers.

On election night, they deluged Democratic caucuses with 239,000 people — almost double the 122,000 who attended in 2004 — and Obama came away with the win (albeit, the prize was 16 delegates versus the 14 Clinton won by placing third.)

In New Hampshire, Obama would have to repeat the feat. This time, however, Kerry's old field organization was lined up on the Clinton side, as were the leaders of both houses in the legislature and most of the party establishment.

Most of us watched Iowa vote on television. What we saw was a media spin on the returns, a parsing of "entrance polls" that showed Obama winning, as the commentators put it, "across the board."

He won handily among men, split the women, and even beat Clinton among women under the age of 35. When the results were broken down by age, Obama's support among voters ages 18 to 24 was astronomical. If 45 is the new cut-off age between young and old voters, Obama took

50 percent of the young voters against Clinton's 16 percent.

The Iowa returns, the TV pundits all agreed, were a dire warning to the Clinton camp. Projected out across the political landscape, they seemed to show Obama's campaign, which the candidate deftly cast as a crusade for change, was an unstoppable juggernaut.

Before the candidates even climbed on an airplane to fly to New Hampshire, Tim Russert on NBC and George Stephanopoulos on ABC were proclaiming that Clinton would have to completely rethink her campaign.

But there were only five days to do it. One of the unintended consequences of state legislatures leapfrogging their primary dates to get to the head of the pack was that there was no time for thinking.

Waiting On Hillary

When Clinton appeared at her first rally in Nashua Friday morning at 8 AM, she had been awake for 26 hours. The network news teams can move their operation from one state to another simply by switching to a fresh set of correspondents. Candidates cannot. Her campaign stops that day were a fuzzy blur. At many, she appeared tired, defeated and cranky.

On Saturday morning, the *Times* reported the Clinton camp was rife with dissension. "One longtime adviser complained that the campaign's senior strategist, Mark Penn, realized too late that 'change' was a much more powerful message than 'experience.'" wrote Patrick Healy and John M. Broder. "Another adviser said Mr. Penn and Mr. Clinton were consumed with polling data for so long, they did not fully grasp the personality deficit that Mrs. Clinton had with voters." The one thing everyone agreed on was that she would have to recalibrate her image.

But if Clinton was changing her image, the Saturday night *ABC Facebook* debate gave few clues on what the new Hillary would look like. She was, alternately, pedantic, stoic, angry, and wounded ("That hurts my feelings, Charlie," she said when moderator Charles Gibson asked whether she was unlikable.) Through it all, however, she never wavered in her resolve to defend her "35-year record as an agent of change."

The drumbeat to see a new Hillary continued the next day on the Sunday morning talk shows, particularly *Meet The Press.* In his hand, Russert held the latest results of a poll conducted over the two days preceding the Iowa caucuses and the Friday after. It showed Clinton's lead in New Hampshire evaporating, wiped out by an Obama surge on the last day. Posting the numbers up for the viewers, he asked a roundtable of political consultants to give Clinton advice on how to change her campaign over the airwaves.

I went over to Nashua High School Sunday for a noon Clinton rally to see how the candidate would react. Outside, 3,000 people waited in a line that stretched a half-mile down the street. A lucky few would get into the small gym that had been set up for the occasion. The others would have to watch on TV monitors in a spillover auditorium and converted classrooms.

Even after the doors opened, the crowd would wait. Clinton was more than an hour late. She was at the time still huddled in a hotel room getting advice — from advisors in the room as well as those on TV — on how to change who she was.

Howdy boys, I'm back

When I walked into the gym, Channel 7 political editor Andy Shaw was standing at the registration desk. He greeted me with a big bear hug.

"Stump, you made it," he grinned. "Where have you been?"

Before I could unlock his grip, his counterpart at CBS Mike Flannery came up, but not to see me. "Hey Andy," Flannery said. "You guys have the best neck ribbons. You put us to shame." He pointed to the red, white and blue lanyard holding Andy's credentials. "Can you get me one?"

"We have hats too," Shaw said.

Swag? They were singing my song. "I'll take one," I said.

"All they say is Vote 2008," he said.

"Forget it," I said. "I thought they might say POOBAH or PUNDIT or something."

Roger Simon, another old Chicago friend, was sitting alone on a folding chair busily typing on his laptop. This year, Simon is the chief political correspondent of *Politico.com*, the Internet start-up that is like a traveling All-star team of political pundits, and he too greeted me warmly. Making small talk, I noted that every time I saw him at a campaign event, he was typing up a story for the web.

"Yeah, we're all wire service reporters these days," he said.

Chris Matthews of *Hardball* and Mort Kondracke of *Fox News* showed up, as did all of the major newspaper reporters and columnists. Soon enough, Russert walked in. I took the occasion to ask him a question that had been on my mind all week. "Do you sometimes feel like you're leading the story instead of following it?"

"Leading the story?" he asked back.

"Yeah, leading the campaign story. Your program is so integral to it all—"

"I never thought of it that way. I just ask the questions," he answered. "That's my job. I ask tough questions. If they can't answer tough questions, then they aren't prepared to make tough decisions."

I stayed at the rally as long as I could, but I had a book signing I couldn't miss at the Toadstool Bookshop in Milford so I defer here to an account of Clinton's performance by Simon, the only reporter in the room who was paying attention:

Clinton talked about issue after issue in almost mind-numbing detail and answered question after question in an event that lasted more than an hour and a half.

But Clinton's crowd was much smaller at the end of her speech than at the beginning. Hundreds of people trickled and then streamed out while Clinton was still talking. But she went on and on as if she did not mind. And maybe she didn't.

"You campaign in poetry, but you govern in prose," Clinton said, quoting Mario Cuomo. In other words: Dull is good. Dull is a sign of competence. But can dull get you elected? Especially when your chief rival is selling poetry?

"I applaud his incredible ability to make a speech that really leaves people inspired," Clinton said of Obama after her speech. "My point is that when the cameras disappear and you're there in the Oval Office having to make tough decisions, I believe I am better prepared and ready to lead our country.'"

An Alternate Reality

On the Republican side of the fence, I felt an obligation Monday to go see Mitt Romney just to get a fair and balanced perspective.

I caught up with him at a monthly meeting of the Rotary Club in the Nashua Country Club. Before Romney's speech, the club president greeted us, the attending national press, with a rousing rendition of its famous Hello

Song — *Hello, Hello, Hello . . . The most beautiful word in the world is Hello* — and asked us to join with him in singing the national anthem led by Jarrett Jackson, the only black person in the room, a waiter.

Romney is not exactly on what you'd call a roll. Despite spending $24 million on TV ads, his campaign is a hair's breadth away from tanking. So with a salesman's ease he's unveiling today a new theme (and new graphics) centered around, you guessed it, change.

In a dining room set with white linen tablecloths and overlooking the 18th green, he stands next to a huge TO DO list that looks like a blown-up post-it note. The new message is that "Washington is Broken" and it can't be fixed by the same old Washington insiders (read John McCain) who live there.

The gist of the speech is a Babbitt-like rendition of the 13-points on his TO DO list. They are a laundry list of Republican catch phrases: Make America Safer, End Illegal Immigration, Reduce Taxes, Cut The Pork, Better Care for Veterans, End Dependence on Foreign Oil, Make Government Simpler, Fix Social Security, Strengthen Our Families, Balance The Budget, etc.

When Romney finishes, there is only polite applause. "Sounds to me like a PowerPoint presentation," I whisper to Ron Brownstein, political director of the *National Journal*. "Actually, he's done those," he says.

A Note on Technology

The distance from the Nashua Country Club to Romney's next stop at the Salem Elks Lodge is only nine miles as the crow flies but takes about 30 minutes to drive. The route zigzags along former carriage paths between villages, which is one reason why the newest gizmo in the press corps is a Global Positioning System (or GPS).

Regulars on the campaign trail automatically order a GPS from the rental car company. Dumb me, I bought a map. In the parking lot, I ask the CNN truck engineer if he can show me how to get to the next stop. "Don't ask me, I just GPS it," he says.

At the next event, GPS comes up again. This time it is mentioned by a guy who is moonlighting from his job as an IT guru at Romney's national call center in Salt Lake City. GPS, he says, lies at the very beating heart of every candidate's headquarter operations.

To explain: Like all the candidates, Romney has a national call center that uses computer phone software called VoIP (Voice over Internet Protocol.)

For a license fee that amounts to $3 per seat (Skype Pro), Romney employs 100 volunteers a day to make toll free calls to anywhere in America. Free.

When a caller sits down at his workstation, he is fed the day's call list from the campaign's central computer database. It is loaded with the voter registration rolls in every county in America.

One day, the volunteer can be calling the 17th precinct in the 3rd ward in Manchester; the next day, it's the 33rd precinct in 5th ward of Greenville, South Carolina. Whom he calls that day is determined by the high command, which can re-direct the calls at the press of a button.

If the numbskull who answers the phone is willing to talk, the caller tries to extract from him the likelihood that he will vote for Romney. This data is then fed back into the central server, where respondents are divided into five categories:

1) Will Vote For Romney
2) Might Vote For Romney
3) Don't Know
4) Don't Like Romney
5) Won't Vote

The old adage in Chicago politics is "Keep the ones and twos, throw out the fours and fives — and fight over the threes."

But here is where the Romney campaign has taken this to the next level. Through its own proprietary software (leave it to a venture capitalist to invest in software in case this politics thing doesn't work out), programmers can link this data to GPS maps of each precinct.

On Election Day, the central server will spit out a walking around map for precinct workers that shows them the name, address and other information (needs ride to polls) of Romney supporters.

The printout even includes instructions on the fastest route between houses.

"It says stuff like go 200 feet, turn left, ring doorbell at the third house on the left, say hello to Mr. Jones," he said.

Along with the map, workers also are given scripts on what they should say to the ones, twos and threes on their route.

"It's pretty cool," he said.

Tears on the Trail

While I was boning up on Romney's operation, Hillary Clinton was in Portsmouth for a little get-to-know-you session with selected friends at the Café Espresso. It was a coup just to get in. But Marianne Perlong Young was familiar with coups. She'd shaken John Edwards' hand. She was a blurry face behind Barack Obama in a *New York Post* cover photo. And now she had a chance to ask Hillary Clinton a question.

Hillary was late. Two hours late. It was bad enough that Young had to sit and wait; worse yet that she had to do it under the hot lights of a couple dozen TV news cameras.

She was hungry. So was Rob Johnson, the CBS correspondent out of Chicago who was covering the event. They sat down together to eat. She was worried about what question she should ask. She was wavering between asking something about the economy or health care. "Why don't you ask something personal?" he suggested.

And that is the origin of The Question.

"As a woman I know it's hard to get out of the house, hard to get ready. And my question is how do you do it?" Young asked.

The Answer that shocked the world was: "It's not easy. It's not easy," Clinton said, with a moist tear welling in the corner of her eye.

Backlash

I heard about the crying incident on the radio between Romney stops. This was a game changer. I immediately turned the car around and headed back to the Red Roof to channel surf my way around the evening news.

Although the incident topped the broadcasts, the anchors were skittish about placing too much emphasis on it. Some were old enough to remember the famous Muskie tears that ended his campaign in 1972, and the debate that followed over whether they were tears or snowflakes. Others pointed out that Clinton never actually cried (although the video footage clearly shows dewy red eyes.)

With only 22 minutes to recap the day's events, it seemed like a moot point. All of the evening news shows had prepackaged "exclusives" featuring their anchors out on the campaign trail ready to go, and there just wasn't enough time to get into it.

After the evening news ended, the story moved over to the cable news channels. Now there was nothing but time. They played the clip forward and backwards, froze it, zoomed in, and threw it into the graphic bumpers that lead in and out of commercials. Clinton critics questioned whether the Café Espresso appearance wasn't a calculated part of a new strategy to soften Clinton's images. Clinton loyalists pointed out how long and grueling the campaign had been. But neither seemed sure whether it worked to her advantage or disadvantage. In the end, the media consensus crystallized around the notion that it was "a humanizing moment."

When Clinton appeared on *Good Morning America* Tuesday to rehash it with Diane Sawyer, one more thing became clear:

The New Hampshire primary would be a referendum on Hillary's humanity, and the deciding vote belonged to women.

Can The Media Ever Get It Right?

I spent Election Day driving around getting credentials for Clinton's and Obama's victory parties. Oh, how I wished I had that GPS. As soon as I saw the meager spread at the feed tables in the press room at both venues, however, I retreated back to the Red Roof to watch the returns on TV.

The last polls taken before the election gave Obama a comfortable 10-12 point lead going into Election Day. A one-two punch in Iowa and New Hampshire, most of the commentators agreed, would pretty much seal the deal for him. But at 10:31 (EST), The Associated Press declared Hillary Clinton the winner in New Hampshire. For the second time in five days, the Democratic race for the presidency underwent a seismic shift (as the cable commentators called it.)

The most interesting aspect of the evening was that the wire service had to wait until the votes were counted to make the call. The early polls showed Obama would win. The exit polls had shown Obama would win. But no one told the voters. It took more than three hours of counting before, with 60 percent of the votes accounted for, it became clear Obama would not win and the race would move on.

For the second time in five days, the national news networks found themselves reporting on an election that took place in a parallel universe to the one they had prepared to cover. All they really had to go on for much of the night were those flawed exit polls. On the one hand, the exit polls showed that Obama again bested Clinton among young voters under 30 by a margin of 51 to 28 percent. On the other, Clinton regained her edge among women 47 percent to 34 percent. Obama won the independents; but Clinton prevailed among blue collar Democrats earning less than $50,000 a year. And so went the dissection of the data (with very flashy graphics) while everyone waited for the real votes to come in.

In the real election that took place that day something quite different was happening. Over 500,000 people turned out to vote in New Hampshire, eclipsing the previous record of 396,000. Tom Brokaw noted the high turnout on MSNBC and attributed it, in part, to the proliferation this year of media.

"You have to realize we're not the only channel on the air right now. When you have all this media surrounding you, you get excited. Also, with the young people, political commentary on the Internet has grown exponentially. There are so many blogs out there generating interest that it's a new day."

But it was good old-fashioned organization that carried it. The Clinton vote was especially heavy in Manchester and Nashua, two large cities where the Clinton forces deployed most of their army of 6,000 door-to-door canvassers. Obama's hopes for a high turnout on the college campuses never panned out. In a nutshell, Obama lost New Hampshire because the kids didn't turn out.

So the ghost of politics past isn't completely dead, even if The Wayfarer Inn is. You still have to count the votes.

Mr. Bojangles Takes Michigan

January 18, 2008

MITT ROMNEY FINALLY won one. It cost him more than $65 million to do it, and he's gone through more positions than the Kama Sutra to find one that voters like, but Romney won a primary Tuesday, as Gloria Borger observed on CNN, by promising to be the President of Michigan.

The Republican race now moves on to South Carolina where we will see who Romney morphs into next. Before it does, let's review how Romney danced his way across Michigan and back into contention.

It was only a week ago that I watched Romney stand before a Nashua Country Club audience in New Hampshire to announce his prescription for a "broken Washington." Lower taxes, a balanced budget, smaller government and an end to our dependence on foreign oil topped his TO DO list.

As soon as he stepped off the plane in Michigan, however, he added two more items he forgot to tell New Hampshire: a $20 billion bailout for the automotive industry and rescinding the new auto fuel efficiency standards.

Both were welcome news in a state with the highest unemployment in the country (7.4 percent.) It has seen the loss of some 250,000 jobs since 1999, most in heavy manufacturing, and Romney's pledge to rescue the auto industry with government subsidies played especially well against John McCain's straight-backed and straight-talking acknowledgement that those jobs are gone. But the devil in Romney's plan was not in the details, of which there were few, but the missionary zeal with which Romney pledged to help Michigan recover from its "one state recession."

Romney stomped across the state bringing voters the message that this son of Michigan had returned to lead them out of economic purgatory. He visited his old elementary school teacher (but not his private high school alma mater Cranbrook Academy), huddled with an unemployed mother who hopes to retire to Florida (a staffer's mom), and stopped by the state Capitol to pay a teary homage to a portrait of his father, the late Gov. George Romney, just days after Hillary Clinton showed it was okay to display a little emotion on the campaign trail.

January 15

Michigan Primary (Romney, Clinton-no delegates)

January 22

Fred Thompson drops out

January 26

South Carolina primary (Obama, McCain)

January 29

Florida primary (McCain, Clinton-no delegates)

Michigan was Romney's home turf — he pointed out to all who would listen — even though he left the state in 1965 at the age of 18. He knew they call soda "pop" here; they think they speak without an accent; and they all believe they have the automotive industry in their blood. Romney talked to the Michigan voters like he'd been sitting around the garage with them all these years bemoaning the demise of the old Hemi engine and now, dad gum, he was going to do something about it. And they swallowed this corn, even though it was a very different Romney who started this quest a year ago.

Sounding more like the Bain investment banker he is (he made his fortune backing start-up companies like Staples and Domino Pizza), Romney scoped out the Republican field and decided all you needed to run for president was a good business plan. He had no natural base, but he had achieved some mild repute for successfully pulling off the Salt Lake City Olympics, which he then parlayed into a single term as Republican governor of Massachusetts (running on a pro-choice and pro gay rights platform). His strongest attribute was that he was a telegenic businessman whom nobody knew much about; and his ace in the hole was that he had a personal fortune of $280 million he could pour into making his image into whatever he wanted.

When Romney surveyed the political landscape, he saw it as a marketplace of ideas. If he could recast himself as a social conservative, strong anti-terrorist and fiscal disciplinarian — the so-called three-legged stool of Reagan Republicanism — he could occupy prime space in the Republican party mall. He could define himself there in the early primary states through early television advertising and make minor adjustments based on how the market responded to his appeal.

Romney is not the first businessman to fancy that America might benefit from his business acumen. Steve Forbes, Ross Perot, Wendell Willkie and Romney's own father come to mind. All follow in the footsteps of Herbert Hoover, the last business genius to successfully win the office in 1928 — just prior to The Great Depression.

One reason businessmen are singularly unsuited to politics is that they tend to think of politics as a self-correcting marketplace. By studying the economic and moral forces at work in the consumer's mind — Romney fondly calls it "looking at the data" — they believe they can fashion a campaign, a set of positions or, as it were, "a product" that a majority of voters will buy.

The hothouse nature of campaigns, however, often skews the data. Controversies arise out of nowhere to dominate debates; external events suddenly shift the issues; and the media, especially in this day and age, throw wildcards on the table when they are least expected. Successful politicians navigate their way through the game more by instinct than plan, with a certain trust that voters will come to find in them their core values. But a man with a plan doesn't give it up easily, or, as in Romney's case, elegantly.

The underlying fallacy of this business-like approach to politics is that nobody is buying anything, really. Voting is free. There is no guarantee people will vote their self-interest or even recognize it in a candidate. More often than not, voters choose to cast their ballot (or not) on personalities or for reasons that don't become apparent until the exit polls are in; and sometimes, elections are won by happenstance. In Michigan, for instance, it can be argued the biggest factor in Romney's win was a winter snowstorm that discouraged independents and Democrats from turning out for McCain.

As late as last December, when the race was still confined to newspaper columns, blogs and Sunday morning TV talk shows, Romney's run was going as planned. He had comfortable leads in both the Iowa and New Hampshire polls. If events played out that way, the momentum of two early wins would make him all but unstoppable, the pundits said. Then the voters started having their say.

For all the money Romney spent in Iowa on television advertising — $8 million, 20 times the amount spent by eventual winner Mike Huckabee — he couldn't stem the surge among evangelicals for the likable Baptist minister from Arkansas. Early on, Romney miscalculated that his true opposition was Rudy Giuliani and went after him for being soft on immigration. Later, taking the advice of his own consultants to "go negative," he aired commercials attacking Huckabee in Iowa and John McCain in New Hampshire, both of whom benefited from Romney's tacit acknowledgement of their strength.

By the time he got to New Hampshire, Romney was dancing around his own positions. His stump speech sounded remarkably the same from locale to locale, but the items on his TO DO list subtly shifted up or down depending on the audience he was speaking to. The sudden assassination of Benazir bhutto in Pakistan reminded voters of America's fragile role in the Middle East, and Romney's slim credentials in that arena. So, ripping a play from Barack Obama's playbook, he came up with the theme that Washington needs fundamental change, and "the same old Washington insiders (read John McCain) can't change it."

I admit to being baffled by how Romney can run as a Republican promising change in Washington. Isn't the current president a Republican? And didn't the Republicans control both houses of Congress for six of the last eight years. (And isn't Romney's biggest backer in Illinois former House Speaker Dennis Hastert, who presided over the House?) The health care stalemate, the earmarks, the ballooning federal budget, the loss of American prestige abroad and decline of the automotive industry at home — all the things Romney promises to fix — took place on the Republican watch.

But Romney got away with it in Michigan. One reason, exit polls showed, is that, even among Republicans, President Bush enjoys only a 53 percent approval rating. Another, clearly, is that Romney significantly outspent his rivals on television advertising in Michigan — $2.1 million versus $554,000 by McCain and $346,000 by Huckabee — most of it highlighting the Romney family's long connection to the state, which was "a strong factor" in the decision of 58 percent of the people who voted for him.

So Romney is back in it. The leader, in fact, as the delegate count goes; and the only Republican candidate, except Giuliani, with enough money to advertise in the critical primaries ahead.

He got there on a hoof and a smile, waltzing across a depression economy promising that Michigan's famous "Can Do" attitude will carry the day. You can have all the business plans in the world, but in the end, nothing beats pandering in American politics.

"Tonight proves that you can't tell an American that there's something they just can't do," Romney told supporters at his victory party, "because Americans can do whatever they set their hearts on."

And if you believe that, I've got an old Rambler I want to sell you.

Air Wars vs. The Ground Game

February 1, 2008

SAY GOODBYE TO the ground game. The days of house parties in Iowa and coffee shops in New Hampshire are over, and all the churches in South Carolina have voted. With Super Tuesday looming ahead, the presidential race now moves to the air and the battlefield has widened, considerably.

On Tuesday, 23 states will hold primaries or caucuses. They will bring out about 20 million voters in states where the absentee ballots alone already exceed the total votes cast in Iowa, New Hampshire, Wyoming, Nevada, and South Carolina combined.

This is the phase of the campaign when retail politics gives way to mass communication. That is usually defined as a wave of political spots just before Election Day that wallpaper our television sets making the candidates about as ubiquitous as the Empire carpet man. But this is anything but a usual year in politics. This is a year that stretches the imagination of even the best political pundits.

January 30

Edwards, Giuliani drop out

February 3

Obama raises record $32 million in January, 88% online

February 5

Super Tuesday

"They call us the Best Political Team on television," John King confided to colleagues on CNN during the New Hampshire primary, "but I've covered six presidential campaigns and I've never seen anything like this."

Where Are We Now

We have reached this point in American politics on the back of too much money seeking too much influence.

Hillary Clinton and Barack Obama started the game with $100 million in their kitty. John McCain raised and spent $35 million before he decided to go it alone. Mitt Romney has shelled out $80 million so far ($35 million from his own personal fortune) just to stay in the race and says he's willing to spend another $40 million to get another Olympic gold or two. (Montana is still up for grabs.)

But it's not a money game this year. McCain-Feingold, the hard-fought 2002 campaign reform bill aimed at taking money out of politics, is so last time around. Even McCain doesn't mention it on the campaign trail. Feingold. Who's he?

This year, the money seems to take care of itself.

This year, it's war.

The Generals

The battle lines have hardened between the Clinton and Obama camps.

While the candidates hopscotch across the country ginning up photo ops for the 24/7 news cycle, the campaign headquarters for both are bustling with field organizers, media planners, Internet specialists, call center volunteers and other below the radar campaign workers who handle the mundane mechanics of a campaign.

To a large extent, the headquarters operations are reflections of the top strategists in each camp, Mark Penn for Clinton and David Axelrod for Obama, who are the Rommel and Patton of this war. The Clinton campaign runs out of headquarters in Washington, where Penn is the consummate insider. When he is not dabbling in politics, he is the unlikely CEO of Burson-Marstellar, one of the world's largest public relations firms. He is a master of polling data and his approach to politics is hardly a secret. He recently authored a book — "Microtrends: The Small Forces Behind Tomorrow's Big Changes" — that argues "there is no One America anymore, or Two or Three or Eight. In fact, there are hundreds of Americas, hundreds of new niches made up of people drawn together by common interests."

Axelrod has planted Obama's headquarters in Chicago, where his roots go back to his early 80's days as a political reporter for the *Chicago Tribune*. Inspired by a stint as press secretary in the campaign of the late Illinois Sen. Paul Simon, he gave up journalism to become a political consultant and has had a hand in all the major races in Illinois for the last 20 years, including Obama's Senate run and five campaigns for Mayor Richard M. Daley. His gut feel for what people are thinking, coupled with smooth commercials that sell his candidates as just like you, has won his firm work across the country for, among others, Senators Clinton and Edwards. [see Jonathan Alter's column in Newsweek January 21, 2008 for a more astute comparison of the two.]

While Penn tries to stay out of the campaign limelight, Axelrod's finest moments often come on the campaign trail where his trenchant analysis of the political landscape makes him a welcome guest in the press spin rooms. One recent example, his comment to *New York Times* reporter Adam Nagourney three days ago on the race so far:

"This race requires everyone to sort of throw away their old assumptions and start thinking anew. The important thing is to measure on Feb. 5 where we are in terms of delegates. My guess is one of us will be ahead, but not decisively, and one of us will be behind, but not decisively, and this will go on for a long time."

The Troops

Neither Penn or Axelrod immerse themselves in the mechanics of a campaign. For that, they have people. The Clinton camp divides functions among a number of high-profile operatives at the top. Penn, who has been advising the Clintons since 1996, sets strategy with a number of outside advisors. Howard Wolfson, her Senate press secretary, handles the media. Karen Hicks is the senior field organizer; and Clinton's old friend and scheduler, Patti Solis Doyle is the campaign manager. Husband Bill, campaign finance chairman Terry MacAuliffe and former presidential advisors like Harold Ickes and Paul Begala also have their own bailiwicks

Obama's camp is more integrated — and fluid. Axelrod relishes the campaign trail action so he relies on his partner, David Plouffe, to run the home office. Plouffe, in turn, has assembled his key operatives based on their special expertise, and their ability to function without a lot of high drama. To Plouffe's credit, he funnels their good ideas up to Axelrod as often as he hands down Axelrod's strategic decisions to the troop. Their office in Chicago looks like a college campus changing classes, collegial and on the move. Axelrod's aim in setting it up, he once bragged to a reporter, was to create a "no assholes" zone.

What both Axelrod and Penn understand is that any campaign strategist worth his salt surrounds himself with good people. In a campaign of this scope, that's a big shaker to fill. The payrolls of both campaigns carry over 1,000 people. Now we will see who has the best salt.

Round One – The Ground Game

The advantage here belongs to Obama, but only slightly. He pulled a rabbit out of the hat with his caucus victory in

Iowa, thanks to a year of advance work establishing a network of local organizers. The Clinton field organization in Iowa was equally as strong, only less successful. “We identified 90,000 potential Clinton caucus goers there, contacted 80,000 of them and turned out 75,000. And we were still swamped,” Los Angeles Mayor Antonio Villaraigosa, a Clinton advocate, complained.

The difference in Iowa proved to be the student vote. Courting their favor, recruiting them to his cause in campus appearances, Obama pursued a strategy that many professionals thought was ill-advised. Howard Dean lost Iowa in 2004 expecting the student vote to carry him in the primary. John Kerry got four million more votes in the general election from young people, but it took a lot of rock concerts just to get them registered. This year in Iowa the students came back early from Christmas vacation, made up 22% of the caucus attendees, and voted overwhelmingly for Obama.

In New Hampshire, it was Clinton’s turn to show off her field organization. She had strong ties to the state’s Democratic Party officials and, at their direction, poured 6,000 volunteers into the streets to bring out her vote.

In the blue-collar neighborhoods of Manchester and Nashua, they turned out a record number of voters while Obama's campus support never materialized.

In South Carolina, Clinton once again relied on the indigenous political organizations — otherwise known as the black churches. She outbid Obama for the support of one key pastor and courted the favor of others (with "love offerings," as they are known in these parts.) But Obama out-flanked her (thanks in no small part to unwitting help from a certain former president.)

Genuine differences in the style of each candidate's field operations rose to the surface in the wake of Obama's South Carolina victory. Clinton has a robust network of field organizers across the country centered in the old school tradition of local party endorsements and union support. Obama's field operatives are more adventuresome — shut out of the black churches in South Carolina, his campaign organized the beauty parlors — and integrally linked to the campaign through the Internet.

Zack Exley, a former Internet organizing director for MoveOn.org, looked into the Obama operation last August and concluded its mix of email, web tools and old school organizing techniques "could rewrite the rules of presidential politics."

"Two things have changed the calculus of presidential primary organizing and now raise the possibility of a hard-fought precinct-by-precinct field battle in states as large as California and as numerous as (the) February 5 primaries and caucuses," Exley wrote. "First, an unprecedented amount of money is now available . . . Second, use of campaign websites now makes hundreds of thousands of volunteer campaign workers available to campaigns in states before a single staffer is hired to work in them. At virtually no cost, campaigns are able to contact those volunteers via email, turning them out to events and trainings and giving them valuable work to do for the campaign in key states."

Obama's key early decision was to hold dozens of three-day training sessions for organizers called "Obama Camp" in Chicago (most aimed at Iowa) and around the country in California, New York, New Jersey, Georgia, and Massachusetts. Specially-selected local volunteers began setting up Obama precinct organizations in each state. They now get maps, instructions, talking points and campaign materials by email, and even have their own blogs and Facebook community.

The names of volunteers who sign up for the campaign on Obama's website (the chief source of campaign help) are instantly dispatched to the nearest field operations center. Within minutes, literally, a volunteer receives a personal email from an organizer that links him or her to a dozen or so ways to participate in the campaign. Mobilizing this field organization to work targeted congressional districts this weekend is a key to Obama's Super Tuesday strategy.

Round Two — The Air Wars

In the halcyon days of 2007, when both campaigns were flush with money, Super Tuesday was supposed to be a mopping up operation. Momentum from a string of early primary wins was supposed to carry a frontrunner into the big states where a last push of television advertising would bring in enough delegates to put him or her over the top and drive opponents from the field.

But the early primaries did not go as expected. With only $25 million left in the war chest, the Clinton and Obama campaigns are now faced with the prospect of buying advertising time in 21 of the 50 most expensive media markets in America, including New York (#1), Los Angeles (#2), Chicago (#3), Philadelphia (#4), San Francisco (#5), and Boston (#6).

Time buying for political ads on television is a stock in trade of politics, with the calculation of what to buy as tricky as everything else in this campaign. It's not based on the standard cost per thousand viewers (CPM), or even cost per thousand voters. The calculation this year comes down to cost per delegate — in a political landscape where Clinton and Obama are almost sure to split evenly the delegate totals in half the places they are competing.

The Problem in a Nutshell

The problem in a nutshell is two-fold: 1) Democratic party rules award delegates in a state to the candidates based on the proportion of the votes they receive; and 2) within each state, two thirds of those delegates are divided up based on how each candidate does in each congressional district. In congressional districts with an even-number of delegates,

Clinton or Obama will have to win by over 65 percent to avoid a 50-50 split. In districts with an odd-number of delegates (3, 5 or 7), the math says one or the other will gain at least a single delegate advantage simply by coming out on top.

The places where a candidate can pick up the most delegates — for the least amount of TV spending — are smaller states that so far have been untouched by the presidential candidates. In part, this stems from a greater opportunity to define your candidate through television advertising — especially if the other candidate doesn't respond in a timely fashion. That's why Obama launched his Super Tuesday air war on January 18 with buys in Tennessee, Missouri, Connecticut and New Mexico; and why Clinton fired back three days later with buys in Tennessee, Missouri, Arizona and central California.

The War Room

In the war rooms of both camps there are media planners huddled over maps right now plotting the overlays of broadcast markets against congressional district borders. The maps are surrounded by computer terminals.

One is linked to an up-to-date database of all the TV and radio stations in America and the inventory they have available in various hours of the day. Another displays polling data showing where the candidate is running strongest, what groups favor him or her, what TV programs they watch, and what TV or radio stations reach out to masses of them. A third computer connects to a video server where all the campaign commercials are stored. At the press of a button, the media planners can buy the time, select the commercial they want to run, upload it to the TV station's FTP address, and the station will automatically insert it into the program they have purchased.

There are 1,681 Democratic delegates up for grabs Tuesday. Now it's your turn to play. Where do you buy?

The Prize

The big prize is California and its 370 delegates. Along the Eastern seaboard, there are 495 more delegates to be won in a swath of states running from Massachusetts through Connecticut to New York, New Jersey and Delaware. Obama's home state of Illinois has 153 in play. In the South, Georgia, Alabama, Arkansas, Tennessee, Missouri and Oklahoma will choose 352 delegates. Western primaries in Arizona, Utah and New Mexico will pick another 105. The seven caucus states will select the last 203.

One political consultant who does not have a horse in this race says his first advice to both camps would be avoid advertising in the caucus states. Caucuses, by nature, draw only the most-committed party regulars. Political advertising on television wastes money on too many people who don't matter. He would also skip Illinois, ceding it to Obama, and maybe Georgia, if polls show Obama prohibitively ahead. As Obama and Clinton did, he would have started advertising early in the small states. "You have to start two weeks early or you're wasting your money," he says. "The focus has to be on California, New York, New Jersey, and Massachusetts. But that's $10 million easy. It's a huge problem, and I'm glad I don't have it."

California Dreaming

California is so big and sprawling, it's hard to know where to start. With 23 of California's 53 congressional districts within signal range, Los Angeles is prime media territory — and costs about $1.5 million to buy for two weeks. One reason to stay out of Los Angeles is that people there have been subjected to so many fundraisers, debates and campaign rallies that a TV spot won't make much difference. One reason for Clinton to go in is to mobilize her support in the Latino community. It's far cheaper for her to advertise on the Spanish language radio and TV there, and more effective.

The San Francisco market, by contrast, is fertile territory for Obama, but it comes with a $1 million price tag and only covers 11 congressional districts. Seven of them will send six delegates to the Democratic convention. The other four will have the odd-numbered five. Those 62 delegates alone, however, are more that can be won in 12 other states holding primaries Tuesday. I would have expected Obama to buy San Francisco. Its liberal, college-educated and large student populations should be his base. But so far, no sign of an ad buy.

Now Sacramento, that's a beautiful place. Clinton and Obama media planners love Sacramento. The city lies in the central valley of California, off the beaten track of the presidential campaign trail. Its TV and radio stations reach into seven congressional districts holding 32 delegates, and it only costs $296,000 a week. The valley is one of the state's most populous agricultural communities, so its farms and orchards are filled with migrant workers, many of whom have settled down as citizens. Clinton has the support of the Farm Workers Union and should do well there. But the valley is isolated from the media-saturated coast, so the television airwaves are a great place for Obama to engage her.

That's the calculation the Clinton and Obama air commanders are making in three California cities. Now imagine, making those same projections in the 21 other states.

Forget Everything I Just Told You

Sometimes this political race moves faster than I can write. That "so far" I wrote so many times before in this piece looked right yesterday.

I awoke today to news that the Obama campaign has made a commercial out of Caroline Kennedy's endorsement, and will run it in New York, Los Angeles, San

Francisco, Philadelphia, and Boston; and on all the cable news channels. That's the same as going all in for $10 million in a Texas Hold 'Em poker tournament. Or, in the metaphor of this piece, dropping an atomic bomb on Hiroshima — and hoping it explodes.

You take your eye off the 24-hour news cycle at your peril this year. In just the last seven days, Obama won South Carolina, McCain won Florida, Giuliani dropped out, Edwards suspended his campaign, and the Kennedys made an endorsement (as did Gen. Schwartzkopf, but that's neither here nor there.)

It was a good week in the news cycle for Obama, and Axelrod played the Kennedy endorsement to the hilt. An op-ed page piece by Caroline Kennedy Sunday in the *New York Times*, a press conference that looked like a family reunion Monday where Ted Kennedy gave his endorsement, and (surprise) a national TV spot Wednesday all but saying John F. Kennedy has from the grave passed the torch to a new generation.

I suspect many weeks of planning back in the campaign office went into snagging the endorsement, and the perfect timing — one week before Super Tuesday — was no accidental news break. On the one hand, it's another illustration of how well integrated Obama's strategy and organization are. On the other, it calls to mind an expression the screenwriter William Goldman once used to describe the movie business in California.

"Nobody knows nothing."

Myself included. But I'm on the outside looking in.

A Split Decision

February 8, 2008

MY CALCULATOR HASN'T seen this kind of workout since my first SAT test in high school. If you are trying to figure out who won the Super Tuesday Democratic contests, you'll want to keep yours nearby. But you can't go wrong this year sticking with the old standby: "none of the above."

Republicans, who cling to the antiquated notion that when you win a state you win it all, seem to have decided that John McCain deserves their nomination — and Mike Huckabee deserves another look. The Democrats on the other hand like a messy democracy. Now they've got one.

Fourteen million Democrats went to the polls Tuesday and the difference in the vote totals between Barack Obama and Hillary Clinton nationwide was 53,000 votes. On the morning after, Clinton had 887 pledged delegates; Obama had 902; and there are 21 more states to hit along the primary trail. The problem is those states hold

February 7

Romney drops out

February 10

Clinton staff shuffle, manager Patti Solis Doyle out

February 12

Potomac primary (Obama, McCain)

only 1,469 delegates — and 2,026 are needed to win the nomination.

To get to that magic number in the remaining primaries and caucuses, one or the other will have to win 76 percent of all the votes to come, a mathematical impossibility under the current system of proportional voting. So the balance of power now shifts to the 796 superdelegates who will attend the Democratic convention in Denver simply because they are party officials, and make up 20 percent of the convention votes.

The Superdelegates

About 350 are senators, congressmen, governors and other "esteemed party officials" — like Chicago Mayor Richard M. Daley and former President Bill Clinton — who get a seat at the convention with no constraints on how they must vote. The other 450 (a delegation larger than California) are little known members of the Democratic National Committee who, in a brokered convention, can be considered the brokers.

Superdelegates are an outgrowth of a particularly ugly floor fight between Sen. Ted Kennedy and President Jimmy Carter at the 1980 Democratic convention. The issue was whether delegates were "robots" forced by the rules to follow the wishes of primary voters. (Kennedy said no, Carter said yes, and Carter won.) Party leaders had been arguing over that issue ever since the 1972 convention, when a rebellious young Afro-haired minister named Jesse Jackson unseated an Illinois delegation led by the deceased Mayor Richard J. Daley. The unruly floor fights tarnished the fall campaigns of Sen. George McGovern in 1972 and Carter in 1980. Party leaders decided to set up the superdelegate system so those with a long-term vested interest in harmony (themselves) would have more leeway in smoothing out the differences between warring candidates. And Democratic conventions have run like clockwork ever since.

The system worked so well that the Republicans have also adopted it. Twenty-three percent (576) of the 2,516 delegates attending the Republican convention in St. Paul (Minnesota) this year will also be superdelegates. While they may not be called on to broker a peace between McCain and Huckabee, their votes could be decisive in platform fights over immigration, abortion and campaign financing, all issues where McCain does not necessarily agree with his party.

In the Democratic race, Clinton and Obama will still have to fight it out in all the states to come — if only to win the news cycle every day over who has "momentum" — but neither candidate will be able to close the deal without the winning over the superdelegates. So "none of the above" remains a pretty good answer, for now.

Back Up For Grabs

If Tuesday's election brought any finality, maybe it will put an end to pundits predicting the race will be over every time another state goes to the polls. It will not.

More attention should now be paid to how Clinton and Obama respond to this uncertain situation. By looking at how the candidates run their campaigns over the next two months you can see how they will govern. There were signals on Super Tuesday in both Clinton's and Obama's Tuesday night victory speeches.

Appearing a few minutes before the California polls closed, Clinton used her national airtime to make one last tactical appeal to West Coast voters who still had a few minutes left before the polls closed. She hit all her talking points, with a promise for every interest group. She came across as a commander-in-chief walking the parapets shoring up her positions against the upcoming siege. She reassured her troops she was ready to lead them forward. But she didn't exactly say in what direction forward lay because no one in the Clinton camp has planned much beyond this night.

Obama, by contrast, gave a speech that sounded like rolling thunder. Having survived the tsunami of Super Tuesday, his vision was clear, his direction unwavering.

"Across the prairies of Iowa . . . from the foothills of New Hampshire . . . to the coast of South Carolina," he promised, "this time is different."

While Clinton prepares for a war of attrition, Obama makes no bones about wanting to build a movement. "Our time has come. Our movement is real, and change is coming to America."

The Road Ahead

In the months ahead, change and experience will fly like flags over the campaigns of Obama and Clinton. And forward they will march. The Potomac Primary, a collection of three previously ignored primary contests in Maryland, Virginia and Washington, D.C., is the next Tuesday contest. The Wisconsin primary is February 19. Texas and Ohio are March 4. Pennsylvania seems ages away on April 22. And don't forget Montana at the tail end of the primary trail June 3.

A messy democracy? Meet the Democratic Party. But who would want it any other way?

Scenes From a Foregone Conclusion

February 22, 2008

OLD CITY EDITORS **never die.** They just haunt you from a distance. I learned that the hard way when I picked up the phone and found at the other end Bob Wills, the former city editor of the Milwaukee Sentinel.

Wills, at 81, is supposed to be safely retired in Nevada. But that doesn't mean he isn't following this election.

"So what do you think? Obama has won eight in row. Does that mean it's over?"

"Not until Wisconsin says so," I said.

"What about the Republicans?" he asked.

"I heard John McCain bought out the Fish Fry at Serb Hall. He's the featured speaker at Ronald Reagan Day."

"What the heck is that?"

"It's a chance for Republicans to go after Reagan Democrats in a union hall with bowling alley," I said.

"Can McCain bowl?"

"I don't know," I said.

February 19

Wisconsin primary (Obama, McCain)

February 24

Ralph Nader says he will run as an independent

February 26

Oil price tops $100 a barrel

"Well, get your butt up there and find out," Wills said. "And stay away from the speeches. We need more human interest."

Ronald Reagan Day at Serb Hall

Ronald Reagan Day is not an official national holiday. You cannot, for instance, buy furniture at a discount on it. But in a year when Republicans are hungry for some connection to the good old days, Reagan Day at Serb Hall is as close as John McCain was going to get to his party base in Wisconsin.

He did not want to be there.

He'd already spent an awkward week sucking up to party conservatives at the Conservative Political Action Conference in Washington and uncomfortably accepting Mitt Romney's grin-and-grip endorsement before Romney closed down his campaign headquarters in Boston. The game was over. The prize was won. But Mike Huckabee refused to cry uncle.

So here McCain was, standing outside the Friday fish fry—only 20 minutes away from a flight back to Arizona for a little rest and relaxation away from the campaign trail — gazing at a portrait of Lance Sijan, a Serbian American pilot shot down like McCain flying a mission over North Vietnam in 1967.

For a few moments, the Republicans would have to wait. McCain read the inscription next to Sijan's Congressional Medal of Honor citation. After being shot down, Sijan called in rescue helicopters for his crew then slipped into the jungle for 46 days to avoid enemy search teams. He was captured once, escaped, captured again, tortured, put in isolation and shipped to Hanoi, where he died in a North Vietnamese prison.

The plaque reminded McCain of a story, not his own, but the story of Mike Christian, a farm boy from outside Selma, Alabama, who was McCain's cellmate in North Vietnam. It was a story he often used to close speeches. Looking ahead to the shifting political landscape and the arguments he would now have to make as the Republican nominee, he knew he wouldn't have much occasion to tell it again soon. So this was the time and this was the place.

The 450 assembled Republicans, many of whom had been aligned with Romney or were Huckabee fans, waited to be won over. McCain knew he had to give them what they came for so he did: a promise to rein in federal spending, secure the border, appoint conservative judges and fight radical Islamic extremism.

On Iraq, he praised Gen. David Petraeus and the surge promising, under a McCain regime, "I will never, ever, surrender. They will." And that brought him around to Sijan and Mike Christian.

"From scraps of red and white material with a bamboo needle," McCain told the crowd, Christian sewed a small American flag inside his blue prison uniform. "And every evening, we would take out Mike's shirt and say the pledge of allegiance."

."Now he wasn't doing that because it made him feel better. He was doing it because he knew how important it was to us to pledge our allegiance to that flag," McCain said. "And I'm happy to tell you there are so many Mike Christians of that era and now that we will win this struggle with radical Islamic extremism, and they will help us make America what Ronald Reagan always envisioned, a shining city on a hill. Thank you very much."

A moving moment. But is it enough this year to be elected president?

Depression in Wisconsin

Wisconsin is depressed. The people are dispirited. The Packers lost. And there's another snowstorm coming in tomorrow. Perfect weather for Wisconsin Democrats to decide who should lead their party into the fall elections.

I attended my first gathering of them Saturday morning at The Brat Stop in Kenosha where they turned out 1,500 strong to welcome Hillary Clinton to the state. They filled every inch of the space, the balconies and the dance floor, waiting in folding chairs, bundled in sweatshirts and parkas to ward off the cold drafts coming in from open doors. In the rafters hung banners for their favorite teams — The Cubs, The Bears and The Packers — symbols of their despair.

They were laid off factory workers, retirees whose pensions had been snatched out from under them, the infirm drawn by Clinton's promise of universal health care, and students who dropped out of community college when their money ran out. There were so many more of them waiting outside that the fire marshal closed the doors to avoid exceeding the room's capacity.

Clinton was bringing to Wisconsin her "Solutions for America" speech, a compendium of government programs she had sponsored or would sponsor to bring the American economy out of the doldrums of the Bush-Cheney years. Her message could not have been more timely.

In the *New York Times* that morning, it was reported that consumer confidence in America has dropped to its lowest point in sixteen years. Automobile sales are at their lowest point in ten years. American manufacturing, where some one in eight jobs are linked to the auto industry, is on the skids. The construction industry is in the tank. The cost of oil imports is up 67 percent from only a year ago, and food and health costs are on the rise.

For Wisconsin (and Ohio next week) Clinton has wrapped these dire statistics into a populist appeal to "the hard-working middle class" who struggle to make ends meet while the fat cats on Wall Street, the investment bankers and corporate CEO's enjoy windfall profits and tax breaks. Every line is red meat to this crowd. They cheer wildly and break into chants of "Hill-a-ree!" after every dig at their oppressors. They even cheer New Jersey Governor Jon Corzine, who is traveling with Clinton, when he introduces her as "The First Lady of Solutions" — apparently unaware that before his sojourn into politics Corzine made $300 million as chairman and CEO of the investment firm Goldman Sachs.

But this crowd wasn't there just to cheer. Everyone there, it seemed, had come as a supplicant to find out what Clinton could do for them. There was an IT guy who lost his job to a programmer from India and wanted to know how to keep "them" out of the country. A former Marine who wanted Clinton to look after his buddies in Iraq "then look out for me here." A student who wanted more money for colleges so she could pay lower tuition.

And then there was 11-year-old Jade Bailey, who'd waited two hours so she could thrust her hand up to ask a question. "What are you going to do for people who don't have a house or enough food?" she asked.

"Do you know someone who is losing her house?" Clinton responded.

"Yes, my mother is," she said.

Say what you will about Clinton's cold and calculating campaign, she has the right instincts. She asked Jade and her mother Donna Bailey, 42, to step up in front of the crowd and tell their story. Donna said she was a hairdresser, but because of hard times, people weren't asking for the perms and dye jobs that kept her going and she was having a difficult time finding a second job. They live in an $87,000 home Bailey bought on an adjustable rate mortgage with payments that recently jumped from $600 to $1,000 a month, so the home is now in foreclosure.

The familiar story of the sub-prime mortgage crisis dominates the headlines. Sure enough, Clinton has a proposal to solve that too. She would freeze foreclosures and provide government-assisted workout plans. But she also has the good sense to give Bailey the business card of a local Democratic official, whom she asked to help fix Bailey's problem.

Solutions are like that sometimes. They work best one problem at a time. And when you offer all the solutions in the world at the same time, you're not solving problems; you're giving a speech.

Meanwhile, Back in Milwaukee

I'm staying at my brother's house in Milwaukee and the phone is strangely silent. Four years ago, it was ringing off the hook in the Wisconsin primary with robocalls from local officials endorsing their favorite presidential contender. So far this year, nothing. There is an occasional political commercial on TV: Obama complaining about corporate executives who make more in ten minutes than you make in a year. Clinton wondering why Obama won't debate her. But it's a light buy. (867 spots for Obama against 285 for

Clinton in the Milwaukee market, according to the *Journal Sentinel*, versus the 4,000 each ran in New Hampshire this year.)

In a conference call with reporters, Harold Ickes, a Clinton delegate strategist, explained why. By his reckoning — a post-Super Tuesday reckoning that contradicts his previous reckoning that Clinton would sweep it — there is no way either Clinton or Obama will win the nomination at the end of the primary route. Even after Wisconsin, Texas, Ohio, and Pennsylvania check in, right up to the last contests in Puerto Rico and Montana, Ickes figures that Obama will be 340 delegates short of a winning majority at the Democratic convention while Clinton will need only 480 — a 60-delegate difference. That makes the 796 superdelegates pivotal for both contenders.

Using their own crude (and varying) methods, the major media outlets have come to the same conclusion. So the smart political reporters this week are scrambling to find the superdelegates, interview them and write about the battle to woo them.

The rest of us are in Wisconsin. But it's so boring the Democratic Party's Founders Day Dinner featuring back-to-back speeches by Clinton and Obama turns into a debate over who first coined the phrase "Just Words." Nothing is more boring that two politicians discussing grammar. So when the politics get boring, the bored go bowling.

Bowling with The Huckabees

Sleet and snow covered Wisconsin Sunday night when I pulled into the Olympic Lanes on Milwaukee's south side. Bad weather forced Hillary Clinton to cancel her upstate rally in Wausau. Barack Obama couldn't make a meet and greet in Kaukana so he secretly flew off to North Carolina to break bread with John Edwards.

But all was warm and cozy at the Olympic Lanes, brightened, perhaps, by the tan on Mike Huckabee's face. Huckabee was newly returned from giving a speech to Young Republicans in the Cayman Islands — Hey, a guy's got to make a living. Now he was ready to dive back into his race for second place in the Republican nomination sweepstakes.

He and his wife Janet are here at the invitation of Don and Beth Minikel, a Racine machinist and his Sunday school teacher wife. Since December, the Minikels have been the Wisconsin coordinators of Huck's Army, a loose-knit array of volunteers organized through meetup.com, and pretty much the entire Huckabee field organization in the state. They spend their evenings making buttons and hand-lettered signs for Huckabee at their kitchen table and their weekends making phone calls to friends, canvassing their neighborhood and putting up Huckabee signs wherever people will let them. If you are going south on I-94 to Chicago, look for the red barn at the state line curve to see their handiwork. They believe in Huckabee because he shares their values.

"God in his wisdom has given him to us," Beth says. "He's the only candidate running this year on faith."

The Minikels have gathered 100 friends and other Huckabee volunteers to greet him. More than a few have brought their own bowling pins, photos and mementos they hope Huckabee will autograph. Huckabee will make no speeches. He doesn't have to. All he has to do is step out on the alley with two fingers and a thumb in a ball to make the front page of newspapers the next day.

So tonight is all fun. A Huckabee Special. When Janet steps up for a practice round, the sound system is playing a country song — "She's a good hearted woman in love with a good timing man," by Waylon Jennings. She knocks over four pins. Huckabee eats pepperoni pizza as he bowls and, at random, picks out reporters to bowl a frame against him. When one tries to beg off because he's not wearing the right shoes, Huckabee chides him, "We'll never tell. Just do badly. That's all we ask."

He points to an audio engineer to go next. He hands him the ball and puts the headset that the guy usually wears over his own ears. Next he beckons over Joy Lin, a CBS embedded reporter who has followed him around with her little camcorder since their earliest days together on the trail. Exchanging places, he pushes the camcorder into her face. "Here, I'll do you like you do me," he says.

The whole evening lasts a little over an hour, and the Huckabees don't leave until they've autographed every item presented to them. History may soon record that Huckabee's run for the presidency ended in a bowling alley in Milwaukee; but that is also where the Christian Coalition found a new leader. A fun one.

Anatomy of an Obama Rally

Barack Obama's best day in Wisconsin was probably his first. On the night of his triumph in the Potomac primaries of Virginia, Maryland and the District of Columbia, he appeared before 18,000 students in Madison's Kohl Arena to deliver his "Stand for Change" speech. He would give the speech again, many times, to packed auditoriums on campuses in Oshkosh, Eau Claire, Wausau, Waukesha, and Milwaukee. I somehow missed them all so I drove up on Election Eve to Beloit for his last appearance at Beloit College's Flood Athletic Center.

Beloit is a small town (pop. 36,000) off the beaten path of the campaign trail. When I arrived three hours early, people were streaming onto the campus from as far as 50 miles away, and the story of how they came together is almost as remarkable as the speech.

It began on the Internet last fall when a Beloit College sophomore named Tamara Fouche signed up to become student coordinator of the campus Obama supporters and started recruiting all her friends to the cause. It picked up the day after the Iowa caucuses when the Obama campaign quietly dispatched two field organizers to southeast Wisconsin at a time when most of the media believed the race would be over by Super Tuesday. Then it accelerated to light speed when the candidates arrived last week.

Three days ago, Ron Nief, the Beloit College public relations director, was getting ready to leave for the weekend when he got a call around 2 PM from the director of the Flood Center. There was a woman in the field house from the Obama campaign asking about renting the gym. Although Beloit College had asked Obama to address the students months ago, Nief assumed that was a dead issue. What does she want it for, he asked; when the answer came back "a rally," he swung into action.

Inside of a few hours, college officials and Obama schedulers came to an agreement they would hold a campaign rally 72 hours later on Monday night. It would take several more rounds of conversations, phone calls, IM's, and emails to firm up the logistics of closing off the hall. Secret Service protection needed to be arranged. Media connections had to be set up. Finally, in what proved one of the most elusive details, they had to find a bomb detector dog in Wisconsin to sweep the auditorium. "The campaign people were great. They were easy to work with," Nief said. "Everyone wanted to pitch in."

The first text message to Obama supporters announcing the rally went out at 11 AM Saturday. One of those who received it was Robert Tomarow, a professor of music at the college. He'd been working on a song "It's Our Time Now" for a film project that he thought might be a good introduction to the speech. He called Nief to ask whether it was worth finishing. Nief told him to give it a shot. By Sunday afternoon, Tamarow was in the studio recording the background tracks with Nicole Waters, a local folk singer, who volunteered to sing the lyrics live on stage.

On Sunday night, the Secret Service came around to inspect the hall. An hour later, Obama's staging crew arrived with speaker systems, stages, backdrops, crowd-control barriers and media camera platforms. Fouche meanwhile was emailing, facebooking and texting every list she had to get out the word — and find the 140 volunteers Obama's people said would be needed to staff the event.

On Monday morning, Nief paced the hall wondering whether anyone would show up. The temperature was five degrees above zero. The prediction for that evening was snow flurries with a wind-chill factor of 15 below.

When the college opened the doors to the public at 7 PM, there were 3,000 people waiting to get in. Many had been there since mid-afternoon, so many Nief ordered another field house opened to shield them from the cold. As the hall filled, Obama's field coordinators began selecting out audience members they wanted to stand behind Obama for "The Shot." To create depth of field, the stage on which Obama would speak was set about 15 feet in front of a set of bleachers where supporters would hold up signs. In the camera's eye, this was all the rest of America would see.

The first batch of backdrop fillers included 66 people: 22 men, 44 women, 20 of them black and 10 of them children. Under the direction of an Obama advanceman, they were positioned and re-positioned in the frame — and more were added to fill in the gaps. White-haired people were especially prized and recruited to fill in the front rows. There were standards that had to be adhered to. A woman wearing a sweatshirt labeled FBI was asked to take it off. Handmade signs were replaced with the campaign's blue Change We Can Believe In. But the selection process was remarkably ecumenical.

With the Beloit Memorial High School band playing a medley of their famous fight songs in the background, the gymnasium felt like a giant pep rally. Nicole Waters sang "It's Our Time Now" and, at 9:43, Obama strolled into the hall with no formal introduction — to thunderous applause.

There is a point in Obama's speech where he promises to make college more affordable with a $4,000 tuition credit "but you're going to have to give back something in return," he says. "Work in community service. Work in a homeless shelter. Join the Peace Corps. Do something good. Give back to America and, together, we will move forward."

The response started slowly in the silence after the applause died down. But it grew deafening. "Yes we can, Yes we can, Yes we can, Yes we can."

After it was all over, Ryan Adam, Obama's advanceman, slumped down in a chair just as his Blackberry began buzzing with a new message: "Your travel instructions for tomorrow. Go to San Antonio . . . "

"That's what I love about this job," he told Nief. "You never know where you're going next."

Hope on the Ropes

March 07, 2008

JUST WHEN BARACK Obama thought it was safe to put away petty politics and focus on the fall elections, Hillary Clinton sent a signal Tuesday that it's not over until it's over. Even then it never hurts to put an anvil on top of a Clinton gravestone just to make sure.

Tuesday's primary results in Ohio and Texas did little to alter the delegate race in the slow crawl of the Democratic candidates toward the finish line. But if Clinton can frame her Ohio and Texas victories in the right light, she can re-focus the race in the binocular eyes of the all-important superdelegate spectators and, perhaps, the reporters who are watching them.

It was a stunning turnaround for the New York senator, as she acknowledged in her election night acceptance speech. "For everyone here in Ohio and across America who's ever been counted out but refused to be knocked out, and for everyone who has stumbled but stood right back

February 29

Clinton releases "3 AM" ad

March 4

Texas Primary (Clinton/Obama, McCain)
Ohio Primary (Clinton, McCain)

McCain passes 1,191 delegate threshold

Huckabee drops out

up, and for everyone who works hard and never gives up, this one is for you," she said.

It was also the start of a new rough and tumble phase of the campaign — one where hope now must take a backseat to politics as usual. Obama's promise of "change we can believe in" has taken him far. Soaring rhetoric, astute planning for the complex primary schedule, sharp field organizing and a masterful Internet operation gave his campaign a winning edge and a frontrunner's swagger, especially after the victories started mounting in February.

But just when the Obama Express seemed ready for liftoff, it stalled — brought low in a downdraft of negative advertising. Was he ready to answer a 3 AM phone call? In the pocket of Tony Rezko, the toxic Chicago fundraiser on trial for fraud and bribery? Double dealing the labor movement on NAFTA?

The counterattack on his character should have been expected from a campaign team that invented the term "rapid response." In the range of American politics, it was hardly out of bounds (although a whisper campaign about his Muslim roots and circulation of a silly costume photo were.) The Obama camp was strangely oblivious to the impact of this onslaught and paid the price. Twenty percent of Ohio and Texas voters said they decided on their candidate in the last three days before the election, and most decided in favor of Clinton.

What hurt Obama's image most were not the specifics of the charges, but the growing sense among blue collar voters that he is flying so high that he is out of touch with the everyday concerns of people on the ground about their jobs, health care and a rapidly worsening economy.

Whether or not Clinton has all the "Solutions for America," she at least was offering them up while Obama was more likely to sneak his own program initiatives into a tried-and-true stump speech so familiar to audiences they shout the signature "Yes We Can" response before he even asks the question.

Going forward, Obama will have to step back from all those mass rallies and engage Clinton, yes again, more more debates. He also will have to come out of his corner ready to dirty his hands, and her reputation, with a few counterpunches of his own.

As David Axelrod, Obama's chief strategist, put it after the Texas and Ohio losses, "If she wants to make issues like ethics and disclosure and law firms and real estate deals and all that stuff issues, as I've said before I don't know why they'd want to go there, but I guess that's where they'll take the race."

It is hard to say whom the political landscape favors in the months ahead. There are 12 more contests to go (if you count Guam) with an estimated 5 million more voters still to cast ballots before Montana closes out the season June 3. First up are the Wyoming caucuses Saturday and a Mississippi primary next Tuesday, both likely to go Obama's way.

Then there is a six-week lull before the Pennsylvania primary April 22, a dangerous downtime where every move will be a media play.

Once the battle shifts back to real people casting real votes, Pennsylvania should favor Clinton. It has a similar voter profile to Ohio and, as in Ohio, Clinton enjoys the endorsement of Governor Ed Rendell and the support of much of the Democratic party apparatus.

Clinton forces will emphasize that the 158 delegates up for grabs in the Pennsylvania primary are the largest big state cache left along the campaign trail, the last of many big states where she has run best. But even if Obama loses there, he can look forward to the North Carolina and Indiana primaries on May 6 — where 187 total delegates are at stake — and the Kentucky and Oregon primaries May 20 — where another 103 are in play — confident that the voter profiles in those states give him ample opportunity to offset any Pennsylvania setback.

The irony, of course, is that this seesaw battle to accumulate the last pledged delegates will put neither over the top. Even if Obama or Clinton wins all the remaining states, neither can gain the nomination without substantial support from the 796 superdelegates.

So keep your eye on that grandstand and the superdelegates watching the horses come into the stretch. They are not voters motivated by hope or economic fears. They are governors, senators, congressmen, distinguished party elders and 450 members of the Democratic National Committee who know their way around the track and long ago forswore idealism for the pleasant sensation of standing with their horse in the winner's circle.

A Solution to Florida and Michigan

March 14, 2008

THE SOLUTION TO Florida and Michigan is to let both delegations attend the Democratic convention in Denver this August, but make them all wear dunce caps. Give them T-shirts that say "I'm The Biggest Jackass In The Joint" and hang "Kick Me!" signs on their rumps.

The costumes may not be enough to distinguish them from the other 4,400 delegates. Put a couple American flags behind their ears and Hillary stickers on their cheeks and they'll blend right in. So let's also give them honored guest credentials. That way, they can attend all the important convention proceedings, like the lobbyist parties.

The Florida delegation can still go to the opening reception hosted by the U.S. Sugar Growers Association. The Michigan delegates can travel about between parties in Mercury Town Cars. And they can all partake in the barbeque at ranches owned by Archer Daniels Midland, get

March 6

Obama reports raising $55 million in March, $20 million more than Clinton

March 13

Obama minister Rev. Jeremiah Wright video emerges on Fox News

a free BlackBerry from Verizon, and enjoy all the other perks that go along with deciding the nation's future.

Just don't let them vote. That should not be too much of a sacrifice since it's been almost 20 years since the Democratic Party ever decided anything on the convention floor.

Consider what happened only four years ago in 2004. John Kerry was nominated for president in a half-filled hall on a Wednesday afternoon (with the mayor of Toledo giving a seconding speech) and his running mate John Edwards was officially chosen after his acceptance speech — in a roll call cut short by acclamation at 11:38 PM so everyone could get to their parties.

It is a dubious contention this year that the Democratic convention needs Florida or Michigan to make its nominee legitimate. Even if both delegations are seated, Barack Obama or Hillary Clinton will still need a good percentage of superdelegates to win. That fact alone makes the argument that the voices of Michigan and Florida voters are being muffled a sham at best and, more truthfully, simply a blatant power grab by the Clinton forces. The primary voters aren't deciding this thing, no matter how you cut it. The superdelegates are. But let's look more closely at what those voices in Florida and Michigan said when they did vote.

In Michigan, all of the Democratic contenders — except Hillary Clinton and Mike Gravel — took their names off the Democratic ballot to show their support for the party sanctions. Even then, 40 percent of the Democratic voters who went to the polls chose "none of the above" over Clinton.

In Florida, Democratic party officials pushed their case for moving the Florida primary up from March 11 to January 29 even though they were told, three times, by the Democratic National Committee this would result in the vote not being counted. They filed suit in federal court to challenge the ruling and lost. But they pressed ahead.

Only after it became clear to Clinton that she'd botched her chances in South Carolina did she break her promise not to campaign in Florida; and she still won only 50 percent of the vote versus 33 percent for Obama and 15 percent for John Edwards, who abided by the rules of the game.

Florida Sen. Bill Nelson, the ranking Democrat in the state and a Clinton supporter, says the only fair way to count Florida is to have a redo. "Allowing the massive disenfranchisement of Florida voters to go uncorrected is not in keeping with your responsibility as head of the party," Nelson wrote in a letter to Democratic chairman Howard Dean.

But who was responsible for that disenfranchisement? None other than Nelson himself, who led his party eyes wide open down a blind alley. And he did it ironically, when if he'd left well enough alone, Florida's established March

11 date would have made that state the most important date on the Democratic primary schedule this year.

The debate over whether to seat the Florida and Michigan delegations really isn't about the voters. Any Democrats who went to the polls on Election Day not knowing their vote didn't matter will not win any awards for sharpest knife in the drawer.

The real debate is whether the party hacks who got Michigan and Florida into this bind should be rewarded for their stupidity. There are 53 superdelegates in Florida and Michigan who, as Illinois politician Paul Powell famously said, "can smell the meat a cookin'." And they don't want to be left out.

So let's give them a seat at the table. But keep them away from the knives and forks.

Rethinking Campaign Finance Reform

April 11, 2008

BEFORE THE LULL ends in this endless primary campaign, let's take a moment to think about what Barack Obama and Hillary Clinton have spent just to get to this point. The latest estimates put that at $400 million, about half the $900 million all the Republican and Democratic candidates will spend in this primary season running for president.

In 2002, after a seven-year battle with the entrenched special interests in Washington, Arizona Republican Senator John McCain and Democratic Senator Russ Feingold of Wisconsin put in place a "campaign finance reform" bill that was intended to stop this arms race in political spending.

The McCain-Feingold bill, defeated three times and passed only after the Senate voted 62-38 to break a filibuster, contained the following provisions: Individual contributors

March 18

Obama race speech in Philadelphia

March 25

Clinton admits Bosnia mistake

could give no more than $2,000 (up from $1,000) to a candidate in any election cycle. Soft money contributions to political parties to finance, for instance, their conventions and voter registration drives, would be banned. And the Federal Election Commission (FEC) charged with monitoring all this would have to produce more timely and detailed reports on who gave what to whom.

To keep political spending in check, the FEC also established guidelines for giving federal funds to candidates who agreed to limit their spending in state primaries. Candidates who agreed not to spend over $50 million this primary season were eligible for up to $21 million in federal campaign money; and party nominees who agree not to raise outside funds after the conventions this fall will receive another $84 million for the general election.

A Quaint Notion

In this most unusual political year, this formula for controlling campaign costs seems quaintly out of date. Hillary Clinton and Barack Obama began their campaigns saying they would turn down federal financing; last February

John McCain himself abandoned the spending limits he sponsored and fought so hard to pass.

When Obama can raise $40 million over the Internet in March alone, the $21 million in promised federal funds is not much of a carrot to abide by FEC spending limits. And when the election commission itself can't even get a quorum together to decide the rules of the game, it's not wielding much of a stick. As long as controls over campaign spending remain lodged in the FEC, the argument over campaign finance reform is little more than a theoretical discussion about what mush a toothless tiger can eat.

Activists in both the Republican and Democratic parties were never particularly fond of the McCain-Feingold bill. Conservatives claimed it was a restriction on their free speech (as expressed by money). Liberals decried its limitations on bundling union money and other PAC contributors. The ink was not yet dry on the bill when both sides took advantage of a loophole allowing "issue advocacy" groups organized under section 527 of the Internal Revenue Service code to raise and spend unlimited sums. Thus were born such organizations as the Swift Boat Veterans for Truth and Harold Ickes' Media Fund. Together, they spent $611 million in 2004, bringing the overall cost of that presidential race up to $2.2 billion.

A Matter of Self Protection

The silver lining around the dark cloud of McCain-Feingold is that it forced the U.S. Supreme Court to reaffirm Congress's right to limit the impact of money on elections. "Many years ago we observed that to say that Congress is without power to pass appropriate legislation to safeguard . . . an election from the improper use of money to influence the result is to deny to the nation . . . the power of self protection," Justices Sandra Day O'Connor and John Paul Stevens wrote in their 5-4 majority decision upholding McCain-Feingold in 2003.

"We abide by that conviction in considering Congress's most recent effort to confine the ill effects of aggregated wealth on our political system. We are under no illusion that (the law) will be the last congressional statement on the matter. Money, like water, will always find an outlet. What problems will arise, and how Congress will respond, are concerns for another day."

The underlying facts that shaped the 2003 Supreme Court decision came from a congressional analysis of the 1996 election, when total presidential spending was a mere $630 million (including $234 in public financing). The cost estimates for this year's race start at $3 billion, and go up.

A Modest Proposal: FREE TV

The bulk of all this money goes toward television and radio advertising. Even in a new media environment where millions of dollars are being spent on Internet ads and sophisticated field operations, the Project for Excellence in Journalism estimates that 72 percent of a candidate's advertising dollars this year will be spent buying local TV ads and another 12 percent will go toward purchasing radio time. If the goal of campaign finance reform is to take away the influence of money on politics, why not start by taking away the need to spend 84 percent of that money buying advertising on our public airwaves?

Since 1934, the Federal Communications Commission (FCC) has used its licensing authority over the public airwaves to set rules for the private companies that broadcast on them. Under these rules, Howard Stern can be fined for making outrageous comments, programming inappropriate for children is confined to certain hours, stations are required to air public service announcements, and political candidates cannot be charged anything higher than the lowest advertising rate for their commercials. What if the FCC were also to mandate that a condition for holding a broadcasting license is giving federal candidates FREE airtime in certain periods of the day? We could call it The Public Service Hour and channel what is now a splatter board of negative TV spots into defined parts of the day, just as the British do, where every candidate must make his or her best case.

This is not a far-fetched scenario. In 1996, no fewer than 200 public figures took out an ad in The *New York Times* endorsing "Free TV for Straight Talk." They came from all parts of the political spectrum and included former network anchors Walter Cronkite, John Chancellor, Robert McNeil, Roger Mudd, and Howard K. Smith; former Senators Alan Simpson, Bill Bradley and Paul Simon; and former Republican party chairmen Frank Fahrenkopf and Mary Louise Smith and Democratic party chairmen Robert Straus, Paul Kirk and Charles Manatt.

Two years later, in his State of the Union address, President Bill Clinton vowed "to address the real reason for the explosion in campaign costs: the high cost of media advertising. I will, for the folks watching at home, formally request that the Federal Communications Commission act to provide free or reduced-cost television time for candidates who observe spending limits voluntarily," he told Congress, "The airwaves are a public trust, and broadcasters also have to help us in this effort to strengthen our democracy."

Clinton's resolve crumbled a few days later, along with the rest of his presidency, when a certain little blue dress worn by a White House intern turned up on the Drudge Report. But the president's instincts were right; and his plan would have dampened the current fund-raising arms race.

While We're At It, No Robocalls

Migrating the issue of how to control the influence of money in politics from the FEC to the FCC is not without problems. The countervailing argument to the 2003 Supreme Court decision is a 1976 case, Buckley vs. Valeo, in which the court ruled that while Congress can set limits on candidate fund-raising, setting limits on candidate spending is a violation of free speech rights. That objection, however, has been muted by the explosion of other means candidates can use to get out their message. The Internet, cable TV, direct mail, billboards and, yes, newspapers are all powerful ways to communicate a political message.

Candidates would be free to raise and spend as much money as they wish in these other media. But on the public airwaves, for the public good, they would have to tailor their message to fit in the free airtime slots the FCC rules would prescribe.

And while the FCC is in the mood to get this clutter of political ads off the air, it could use its same powers in the telecommunications arena to let consumers put political robocallers on their DO NOT CALL list. I don't think many of us will miss them.

Change vs. The Special Interests

The watchword on the campaign trail this year is bringing a "change" to Washington that will end the pervasive influence lobbyists have on the political process. That influence derives from the bundled contributions lobbyists for Big Oil, Big Pharma, Big Any Industry can put together to help congressmen, senators and presidential candidates pay for their campaigns — in exchange for little regulatory favors.

Reining in out of control TV political advertising — and replacing it with free airtime — will be a good test of how sincere the candidates are. Because one of the biggest lobbying groups in Washington is the National Association of Broadcasters. Its member stations, the media conglomerates who control them, and telecommunications giants like AT&T that now want to compete with them have so far contributed $54 million to political campaigns in the first three months of 2008.

Giving away air time, instead of selling it, won't go down easy with this crowd. In some battleground states, during election season, political advertising can account for as much as 20 percent of a station's revenues so broadcasters can be expected to put up the fight of their lives to protect that revenue source.

The rest of us, however, would probably welcome the respite. Not only would it drastically reduce the need for candidates to hit up every lobbying group in town to support their candidacy, it would give us back our television sets so we can watch important things, like The Simpsons.

If the candidates mean what they say about taking on the special interests, they'll have to do it one industry at a time, and broadcasting would be an interesting place to start.

No one said change comes easy.

Revenge of The Blob

April 25, 2008

THERE ARE ONLY two ways through Pennsylvania. One is on a beeline across the state on the Pennsylvania Turnpike. The other follows the presidential primary trail from Philadelphia to Pittsburgh with intermediate stops in towns like Altoona, Lackawanna, and, yes, Punxsutawney, where every day is Groundhog Day in politics this year.

Pennsylvanians like to call their domain the Keystone State because it forms the arch connecting the northern and southern colonies, and serves as a gateway to the vast bounty of America. Its squared off borders, which stretch from New Jersey to Ohio, contain a populace that historically got as far as they could in America, and settled for it.

There are two big cities in Pennsylvania—and many small ones. Philadelphia at the southeastern tip is as American as apple pie. Home of the first Continental Congress in 1776, it sits at the nexus of power in the East Coast establishment. Pittsburgh, on the other end of the state, came to prominence more than a century later. Faced with the dilemma of how

April 5

Mark Penn steps down from Clinton campaign after Columbian lobbying revealed

April 6

Obama warns San Francisco fundraiser of bitter people clinging to their guns and religion

April 22

Pennsylvania primary (Clinton)

to exploit their newfound horde of iron, coal and oil resources, the Carnegies, Rockefellers, Fricks, and Morgans built their mills, mines and factories there and filled them with immigrant labor from Europe — Poles, Croatians and Ukrainians, to name the largest contingents — eager to take on the work.

The two cities, as different as night and day, have between them about 60 percent of the Democratic voters in the state. Philadelphia and its four surrounding counties gave John Kerry 1.2 million votes in 2004; Pittsburgh and its three metropolitan counties accounted for another 500,000.

Polls leading up to the primary showed Sen. Barack Obama with a wide lead in Philadelphia and a narrow edge in its suburbs, but they also showed Sen. Hillary Clinton winning by a 3-1 margin among Democrats in the Pittsburgh area.

The winner in Pennsylvania, both sides agreed, would come out of the vast expanse of territory in between: an amalgam of renegade frontiersmen and Quaker, Amish, Catholic, and Lutheran devotees — mostly Republican, but with a fair share of disaffected Democrats — living in small towns that Obama, on the eve of the race, unfortunately characterized as bitter people clinging to their guns and religion.

Debate Fatique

I arrived in Philadelphia just in time for the ABC News debate in the National Constitution Center, the 21st of the campaign. The first person I ran into was a weary Roger Simon, chief political correspondent for *Politico,* who has attended every one.

A poll released that day reported a majority of American people wanted to see the race continue to the very end. "I want their names — and addresses," he scoffed before dumping his laptop at a press table. I asked him whether he was live blogging the event. "That's too easy," he said. "I'm a columnist. I have to make sense of it all."

The first order of business for ABC moderators Charlie Gibson and George Stephanopoulos was to rehash the truthiness of the charges that had been flying back and forth between the Clinton and Obama camps in the six-week lull since the last primary.

Clinton was given an opportunity to correct her claim to have arrived in Bosnia under sniper fire ("I just said some things that weren't in keeping with what I knew to be the case.") Obama, in his turn, was called to account for his "bitter" remarks ("It's not the first time that I've made a statement that was mangled up. It's not going to be the last.")

Just when Obama thought he'd put that issue to bed, Gibson and Stephanopoulos were back at him with a question about his pastor Rev. Jeremiah Wright ("Do you think Reverend Wright loves America as much as you do?"), then another about why he doesn't wear an American flag on his lapel, and another about his association with former Weather Underground leader Bill Ayers. Fifty-two minutes of questions, most about his judgment and character, before a substantive issue was raised.

"It was not a good night for Obama," Howard Fineman commented afterwards on NBC. "It raised questions that will be dragged out over the next months." In the *New York Times* the next day, David Brooks compared his performance to "Michael Dukakis in a tank, John Kerry's windsurfing or John Edwards's haircut." In the spin room afterward, Obama's chief strategist David Axelrod tried to convince reporters the good people of Pennsylvania would see past these distractions. "One good thing about running against Hillary Clinton is that nobody will say that you can't handle a negative campaign," he said.

But the attack had not come from Clinton. She stood on stage grinning like a Cheshire cat while Gibson and Stephanopoulos carried her water. She already had an ad running on TV decrying Obama's bitter remarks; now they were serving up a whole slew of new ways to twist the knife.

When the dust cleared, one thing was perfectly clear. Any notion that the candidates would spend their last days in Pennsylvania debating the issues was gone. This primary would be a test of who could pander most to the pride, patriotism, fears and resentments of the good people of Pennsylvania — that great blob of untamed emotions we sometimes call The American Spirit.

The Morning After

In fact, both candidates had been pandering their way across Pennsylvania for six weeks. Obama downed a Yuengling in Latrobe; fiddled with a Slinky in Johnstown; tasted a chilidog and bowled a 37 in Altoona; fed a calf in State College; sampled homemade chocolates in Lititz; toured a garment factory in Allentown; and nibbled on cheese at Philadelphia's Italian Market. (Thank you, Philadelphia *Inquirer*.) Meanwhile, Clinton toured factory floors in a hard hat, told stories of learning to shoot a rifle with her grandfather at Lake Winola, and knocked back whiskey shots in a Crown Point tavern. At one point, *The Note*'s Rick Klein suggested they forget the rest of the primaries and just settle it all with a chug-a-lug contest.

I caught up with Clinton the morning after the debate at a "Mothers & Daughters" symposium at Haverford College. She arrived with her daughter Chelsea and mother Dorothy Rodham, and she was beaming. "How many of you saw the debate last night?" she asked. All but a few dozen of the 300 women in the room raised their hands. Acknowledging a contingent of students from nearby Bryn Mawr College, Clinton noted that she herself was the recipient of a fine education from a seven sisters school (Wellesley) then launched into a litany of promises (er, solutions) that included equal pay for women, tax credits for child care, more early childhood education, and even a cure for breast cancer.

After she finished pouring syrup on the pancakes, she took a couple crumpet questions. The last was what students should tell voters when they go out canvassing. "Just knock on the door and say she's really nice," Clinton smiled, "or you can put it another way, 'she's not as bad as you think.'"

From Haverford, it was an easy train ride back into Philadelphia where, the next night, Obama would kick off his five-day blitz of the state with a rally before 35,000 supporters on the steps of Independence Hall. But I knew it was time to get off the campaign trail. I'd heard enough of the speeches. Now it was time to listen to the echo.

Driving West

I got in my car and headed west. The road out of Haverford passes through what are considered two good size cities, Lancaster (pop. 55,000) and Harrisburg (pop. 50,000), the state capital. In a shopping mall outside Lancaster, it takes me a while to find six people willing to admit they are Democrats. When I do, five of the six, all women, say they are voting for Clinton. (The lone holdout is a young music store clerk who just moved down from New York.) They cite a comfort level with Hillary, good memories of husband Bill and "experience" as their reasons. An elderly mall walker says she liked Obama at first, but she was turned off "when he insulted us in Pennsylvania . . . and with the minister thing on top of that, I'm going for Hillary." It's a refrain I would hear more than once on my trip across the state.

At Harrisburg, I branch off onto US 22 as it rises up along the Susquehanna and Juniata Rivers into the Appalachian Mountains. For the next 200 miles, the only signs I see of a presidential campaign are roadside placards for Ron Paul. This is where small town Pennsylvania lives, a thousand little dots on the map, sequestered off the highway on even smaller roads.

For all of Pennsylvania's bigness, you forget that most of it is a mountain range. The trees on the hillsides are just breaking bud and the rivers are at their spring high water mark. At Clearfield, where the Appalachians crest, I stop in at a local diner and find myself sitting at the counter next to a young man in a lumberjack shirt. He buries his head in his plate as I banter with the waitress about the primary. When she steps away, I ask him his preference. He looks both ways so as not to be overheard. "Hillary," he says. "But that's because I'm gay, and I really appreciate what the Clintons did for us."

My destination for the evening is Punxsutawney (pop. 6,200), the epicenter of a minor holiday known as Groundhog Day. Getting there puts me on a course of even smaller two-lane blacktops filled with signs warning of deer, Amish horse buggies and drunk drivers.

I arrive well after dark. The only room available is at the old Pantall Hotel. It's almost 10 PM and the hotel bar is closing. The bartender, a student at the community college in nearby Indiana (pop. 15,000), serves up a Rolling Rock and says she will be voting for Clinton. One reason, she says, is that the Obama girl on campus is so pushy and obnoxious she wants to kill her. More to the point, her brother is serving in Afghanistan and she admires how Hillary dealt with disabled vets on a TV show she saw once. "She was so real," she says, "she gets it."

The next morning, I open the *Punxsutawney Spirit,* the local newspaper, to find I'm not the only junkie who's fallen off the political wagon. The day before, Bill Clinton was having dinner with Joanne LuPone just down the road in Brookville (pop. 4,000). Before dinner, he addressed 500 people gathered around her front porch and said, "I love going into small towns. I'm the designated ambassador to small town America for Hillary's campaign."

My reason for going to Punxsutawney — besides buying a T-shirt — was to see Punxsutawney Phil, the ageless groundhog who predicts all things bright and stormy. So after breakfast, I walk across the town square and find him curled up on a rock under cloudless skies with temperatures in the high 70's. He can not only see his shadow, he's basking in it. Sorry folks, looks like six more weeks of campaigning!

The Backside of The Mountain

From the peaks of the Appalachians, the land slopes down into the industrial valleys on the western side of the state. It was here around Titusville that oil was first discovered in America in 1859, and here along the backside of the mountain lie some of the richest iron ore deposits and coal reserves on the planet. Even before the rise of the railroads, the meandering paths of the Alleghany and Monongahela Rivers brought all this natural bounty together in a town called Pittsburgh, where it is made into steel — or was.

In its prime, Pittsburgh supplied almost a third of the world's steel. Blast furnaces bellowed smoke up and down its rivers, steelworkers earned a healthy wage, and unions ran the town. Starting in the 1970s, the steel mills, one by one, began to close. Foreign competition drove down prices, and the unions were reluctant to give back their wage gains (and even that might not have helped). The last of the steelworks closed in the late 1980's.

The recovery was slow and painful. The city's population dropped from a high of 600,000 in 1950 to 333,000. The skyline today is pristine and clear. City neighborhoods are coming back to life. The economy thrives on jobs in financial services, health care, robotics and an array of small fabricating and assembly plants left over from the good old days. I'm anxious to see the transformation, but I still have a few more stops to make along the way.

The Cherry Tree Mine

Just outside Stiffletown (pop. 400), I turn off into the parking lot of the Cherry Tree Mine, an independent coal mine cut into the side of a mountain that no one but the locals know is there. A steady stream of trucks picks up the coal and hauls it 15 miles away to the power plant at Homer City (pop. 1,850).

Tom Dunmire, the mine manager, says the plant is the new face of coal mining in western Pennsylvania. When the steel mills closed, most of the larger coal mines either closed with them or consolidated.

The Cherry Tree Mine opened three years ago to fill the gap by finding smaller veins and servicing local energy companies without the baggage of corporate and union restrictions. The mine employs 108 people. Although it is non-union, wages start at $22/hour with full benefits, roughly the same as larger mines with union contracts.

Dunmire surmises his workers are about equally divided between

Republicans and Democrats. A good number are Iraq and Afghanistan war veterans (and their opinions on the war are similarly divided). Among the Democrats, he sees little support for Obama. "Could it be racism?" I ask. "Maybe there's a little of that," he says. "But there's a lifestyle here that he's just not a part of."

Johnstown

Down the road is Johnstown (pop. 23,000), a regional center known for its hard luck, having flooded not once but three times. The Clinton campaign office is buzzing with activity. A block away, the Obama campaign office is as quiet as a flower shop. A single volunteer makes phone calls while her children draw pictures of the candidate on a table set out with crayons.

Johnstown is represented in Congress by Rep. John Murtha, a 16-term Democrat and Clinton supporter, who has used his powerful position on the House Armed Services Committee to earmark billions of dollars in federal contracts for his district. As a result, in an otherwise conservative area, Johnstown and the surrounding district is almost 2-1 Democratic.

The problem that besets Johnstown, and all of western Pennsylvania, is not the closing of the steel mills. That happened 25 years ago. It's the steady erosion of other light manufacturing jobs lured overseas by cheaper labor costs in a new global economy. There are signs this trend could be reversed. A new Gamesa plant on the outskirts of town employs 150 people manufacturing propeller blades for wind turbines. These are the new "green" jobs both Clinton and Obama say they will encourage if they are the next president.

The larger concern here is that the population is shrinking faster than the jobs are coming in. Over the last six years, it has dropped seven percent; and the median income of the remaining households hovers around $34,000 a year. Emily Cain, a Clinton field worker, says voters here are ripe for Clinton's message of concrete solutions to their problems.

"We've targeted this area," she says, "and we're going to get every vote that's out there." Her counterpart for Obama is not so optimistic — or eager. "Remember, we were never supposed to win Pennsylvania. But come November, we'll know a lot more about this state than we did coming in," he says.

Pittsburgh

The downside of breaking away from the campaign trail is you sometimes find yourself in a city with no candidates to follow. Thus I found myself in Pittsburgh the weekend before the primary with only one event to cover, a Pittsburgh Steelers tailgate party for Obama in the parking lot outside the Steelers stadium. It was hosted by

Dan Rooney, owner of the franchise, and featured five former Steeler greats (Franco Harris, Dwight White, Robin Cole, Ed Nelson, and J.T. Thomas), all talking about how a last minute push for Obama could put him over the goal line.

With the exception of The Steelers — "Don't count Obama out. Dan Rooney is big in this town," a fan tells me — the rest of the Democratic machine in Pittsburgh is lined up behind Clinton. "She got here early and lined up all the important endorsements before anyone knew it would be a race," one prominent Democrat told me. "All you see or hear is Clinton. She's got the mayor, the governor, the women, and the unions. She led the St. Patrick's Day parade. What's left for Obama to get?"

What's left? How about the voters? For their opinion, I went to a mall in a middle class suburb just outside Pittsburgh. And not just any mall, but the Monroeville Mall where George Romero filmed his famous "Dawn of The Dead" in 1978.

The Monroeville Mall

I stood on a Saturday morning at the entrance of the Monroeville Mall intent on gathering 25 straw ballots from Democratic voters planning to vote in the primary. The crowd exemplified Pittsburgh's diversity. They were both young and old, black and white, mothers pushing baby strollers and elderly couples doing weekend errands. To get my 25 Democrats, I had to interview 44 people, 12 of whom were voting for John McCain and seven more who were undecided. The Stump poll, as I call it, came out Obama 13, Clinton 12, with the deciding vote belonging to a young

African-American schoolteacher picking up tuxedos for a friend's wedding.

Here are the top ten reasons people gave to explain their vote:

An African-American mother with child (Clinton): "She was the most poised in the debate."

A middle-aged white man (Obama): "Hillary was already president before. Why should we let her do it again?"

A middle-aged white couple (Obama); "We need a different approach."(wife). "It's change. That's what he's selling."(husband).

An elderly white man (Clinton): "She's been there . . . and that Obama is a little bit of an oreo. You know his middle name is Hussein so maybe he's a plant. That worries me."

A white shoe store manager (Clinton): "She's better for the working guy."

Another African-American woman (Clinton): "She's more experienced . . . and I liked her husband so if we can't have him, she's a good compromise."

Wife (Clinton): "I'm for Hillary because she's a woman and I'm sick of men running this world."

Husband (Clinton): "I'm with her."

Wife: "You better be."

An elderly white woman overhearing (Obama): "I wouldn't vote for her for dog-catcher. I'm for Obama."

A white mother with three kids (Obama): "He's more honest and he's not a mudslinger . . . I don't trust Hillary. I'm a teacher and that's what I teach my kids. He'll be a good role model."

A young African-American man (Obama): "America is in real trouble. We need some fresh ideas . . . and I like that he's a Christian."

I climb back into my car thinking there's no rhyme or reason in what will happen Tuesday. No issues are driving this choice. Not the economy, not health care, not Iraq. Tuesday's primary will be just a good old-fashioned gut check. Who's most like me? And how many "me's" are out there?

The Tide Turns Ugly

On Election Day, the me's turned out in droves, on both sides. Obama came out of Philadelphia's central city with a 130,000-vote lead over Clinton — 30,000 more than his advisors thought would be needed to win the state — and he won a better than expected 45 percent of the vote in Alleghany County, home of Pittsburgh. Then returns from the rest of the state — all those little cities and small towns on the map — started rolling in.

The cumulative effect was the double-digit victory pundits said Clinton would need to carry her campaign forward. She racked up heavy margins around Scranton (74 percent), Allentown (60 percent), Punxsutawney (63 percent), Erie (63 percent), Johnstown (72 percent), and the counties surrounding Pittsburgh (70 percent). According to exit polls, she handily won Catholics (70 percent), white women (68 percent), the less affluent (54 percent) and least educated (58 percent), otherwise known broadly in political meta-speak as lunch bucket, blue collar Democrats.

Over the coming weeks, Clinton supporters will argue to the superdelegates that the Democratic nominee cannot win in November without them (ignoring, of course, the converse: what Democrat would want to win without the college-educated, liberal, young and African-America voters who support Obama?)

But there is a silent killer stalking through this Clinton victory, and it came to light in an exit poll question asking whether race was a major factor in deciding whom you voted for. Fifteen percent of the white voters said it was, and three-quarters of them voted for Clinton.

Call it ignorance, call it racism, call it The Jeremiah Wright factor, but call it for what it is. In that great blob of untamed emotions we call the American Spirit, there's an evil vein of ugliness we have not yet finished mining.

Barack and a Hard Place

May 09, 2008

The victory party was in North Carolina, but the struggle for the hearts and minds of America took place in Indiana — and, up until the last minute, it looked like Barack Obama was losing it.

Hillary Clinton came into Indiana with a full head of steam. In the Pennsylvania primary, she'd proven that a coalition of older, whiter and more rural voters was still a potent force in Democratic politics; and Indiana was filled with them.

By slugging down whiskey shots and tenaciously promising to fight for "jobs, jobs, jobs," a woman who graduated from Wellesley College and Yale Law School, who lived eight years in the White House and owns mansions in Washington and Chappaqua, had suddenly transformed herself into a working class hero; and by bowling a 37 and wearing tailored suits, a true African-American who put himself through Harvard Law School on scholarship and returned to Chicago to organize laid-off steelworkers on the South Side, was cast in the public eye as elitist and out of touch.

New York Times columnist Maureen Dowd captured the dichotomy perfectly:

> *Talking up guns, going to the Auto Racing Hall of Fame, speaking from the back of pickup trucks and doing shots of populism with a cynicism chaser, Hillary emerged from a lifetime of government limos to bask as queen of the blue-collar prom.*
>
> *Just as Obama spent his youth trying not to be threatening, so as not to unnerve whites, Hillary spent her life learning to be threatening so she could beat back challenges to her and her husband — from Republicans and from "bimbo eruptions" and now from a charmed younger rival.*
>
> *As Obama learned to accommodate, the accommodating Hillary learned to triangulate and lacerate. As he learned that following the rules could get you far with adoring mentors, she learned from Bill and Dick Morris and Mark Penn that following the rules was for saps.*

A bad week for Obama got worse when The Rev. Jeremiah Wright resurfaced before the National Press Club to defend himself — and repeat his incendiary remarks.

April 28

Clinton joins McCain call for a gas tax holiday

April 28

Rev. Wright appears at National Press Club

April 29

Obama denounces Wright

May 6

North Carolina primary (Obama)
Indiana primary (Clinton)

The flare-up pulled Obama off the campaign trail in an attempt to douse the flames. Time better spent courting Indiana's voters was eaten up in press conferences and on the morning talk shows fighting a rear guard action against his former pastor.

And then, in what should have been Obama's darkest hour, Clinton threw him a life raft — the federal gas tax holiday.

I went down to Indianapolis Saturday to see how Obama was handling the whole thing. Before I left, I gassed up in Chicago (at $4.09 a gallon) and, around Merrillville, stopped off for a Big Mac (thus blowing the $2.76 I would have saved had I traveled during Clinton's proposed gas tax holiday.)

"The most irresponsible policy idea of the year," Jonathan Alter dubbed it in *Newsweek.* A paltry savings of $30 a person, causing more gas consumption not less, and thus even higher prices from the oil companies, 200 economists wrote in the *Washington Post.*

And a three-runner homer for Obama in that Clinton's plan 1) aligned her with John McCain's bad idea, 2) stole focus from Obama's pastor troubles, and 3) gave Obama a chance to get back on message criticizing cheap political "gimmicks" that could only come out of "the same old politics in Washington."

I expected to find Obama re-energized and on the attack, but soon discovered Saturday was a planned "family day" on the campaign trail, a very well-planned family day set up by a campaign staff that had, up until Pennsylvania, always been two steps ahead in the game.

The schedule called for a noon speech in a suburban high school, a picnic outing in Republican Hamilton

County, a visit to the homestead of his great-great-great grandfather Jacob Dunham (on his mother's side), and a final appearance at an ice cream social in a roller rink in Lafayette. For the first time since Iowa, he brought along his wife Michelle and two daughters, Malia and Sasha, all part of a deliberate attempt to "Americanize" Obama in one of our most red, white and blue states.

Obama's speech at the Lawrence North High School was timed to give networks sound bites for the evening news. It was a low key affair, staged in a small school auditorium instead of a raucous gymnasium, and largely ignored.

But I could feel that something was up. My first clue was a new sign on the lectern that read "Reclaiming the American Dream." My second was a quiet David Axelrod lurking in the back watching reporters react to various lines and phrases.

As Obama waded into his remarks, large chunks of new copy spewed out, all centered on "the dream we all share."

"This economy doesn't just jeopardize our financial well-being, it offends the most basic values that made this country what it is. The idea that America is the place where you can make it if you try, that no matter how much money you start with, or where you come from, or who your parents are, opportunity is yours if you are willing to reach for it and work for it," he said.

"It's the idea that while there are no guarantees in life, you should be able to count on a job that pays the bills, health care for when you need it, a pension for when you retire, and an education for your children that will allow them to fulfill their God-given potential. That's who we are as a country. That's the America most of us here know," he added.

And finally, a quote from Robert Kennedy, speaking 40 years ago in Ft. Wayne. "'Income and education and homes do not make a nation. Nor do land and borders. Shared ideas and principles joined to purposes and hopes, these make a nation,'" Obama quoted Kennedy saying. "And this is still our task today," he added. "In the face of all cynicism, all doubts, all fears, I ask you to remember what makes a nation. And to believe that we can now make this nation again a land of endless possibility where you can still make it if you try."

When Obama came to the part of his speech where he usually relates his own biography — the "improbable" story of the son of a goat farmer from Africa and a woman from Kansas — there were a lot more probable details thrown in: A grandfather who fought with Patton, went to school on the GI bill and bought his first house with an FHA loan. A mother who once had to go on food stamps. A father-in-law, a city worker in the Chicago water department, who, stricken by multiple sclerosis at the age of 30, relied on a walker to get to work "and yet, every day, he went, and he labored, and he sent my wife and her brother to one of the finest schools in the nation."

Reporters covering the speech seized on some of the more red meat quotes for the nightly news. The sea change in attitude and approach went largely unnoticed. Obama's thoughts on what it means to be an American did not jump off the page of the prepared text, and his soft sell delivery did not stir many reporters away from checking their email. But across the span of his remarks, it was clear Obama was doing nothing less than trying to redefine the narrative arc of his own story.

Here, there, and everywhere in Indiana, he was listening to the words voters used to talk about their lives and blending in his own experiences to find chords of agreement that resonated. In none too subtle ways — "this election is bigger than flag pins or sniper fire or the comments of a former pastor" — he was casting off the exotic image of his fiery pastor's robes and his own unusual upbringing and wrapping himself in the Midwestern mantle of a family man who "pumps his own gas."

The new Barack Obama came through in both words and pictures. On the picnic lawn in Hamilton County, he shed his jacket and rolled up his shirtsleeves, playfully smiling while his wife made the introductions and invited listeners to let their own kids play with hers on a nearby swing set. In the Great Skates Roller Rink, he kissed every baby in sight, danced along to the YMCA song and stepped out onto the rink (sans skates) for a touching video of him welcoming his unsteady daughter into his arms.

The next morning, in an hour-long *Meet The Press* interview with Tim Russert, he kept up his low-key demeanor, even during 20 minutes of questions on his former pastor. There was no question he wouldn't answer, and no answer that didn't seem to come from some core values he was proud to profess.

The high-energy charges and countercharges in the closing days of Pennsylvania, his handlers believed, had not served him well. His campaign trademark was the rock star political rally, but last minute attempts to insert digs at Clinton into the flow came across as condescending. "It got kind of sloppy at the end," Axelrod told me. "We held too many rallies and the word we were getting was that Barack seemed to be detached from the people."

Indiana was a chance to correct the record, but the change in style would have to come organically, one day at a time. "We want to close tough here, but we want to close upbeat. We want to show people who Barack really is," Axelrod said.

By the time Election Day rolled around, the Obama campaign was back on track. He did not win Indiana, but, more important, he did not lose it. Clinton won by 14,000 votes (out of 1,275,000 million cast.) The final tally, however, did not did not come in until early Wednesday morning so all that America will remember is that Obama "mathematically" closed out Clinton's quest for the presidency Tuesday night with a decisive win in North Carolina — and Obama delivered another tour de force speech.

In it was a message of hope, patriotism and family values: the opening salvo in Obama's attempt to reshape America's impression of him for the fall elections. It was a message forged in the crucible of Indiana, a hard place for Obama to solve a hard problem, but we will have to wait until November to see if it works.

Dream Ticket or Nightmare Scenario?

June 6, 2008

THE LONGEST AND most expensive primary race in history ended Tuesday not with a bang but a "huh?"

It ended with Hillary Clinton spending three days campaigning in a state that can't vote and Barack Obama claiming the Democratic nomination at the site of the Republican convention.

It ended with a last minute moving of the goal posts, raising the magic number needed to win the nomination from 2,026 delegates to 2,118. It ended with a backroom deal aimed at avoiding backroom deals. It ended with voters in South Dakota and Montana going to the polls to elect 31 delegates, and 60 unelected superdelegates suddenly jumping on the scale to tip the nomination Obama's way.

It ended with a gracious speech by Obama praising the many qualities of his opponent and a flabbergasting, ungracious speech by Clinton claiming she is still a better candidate.

And it ended with Wolf Blitzer blabbing away on CNN about a "Dream Ticket" of Obama-Clinton he first suggested in a debate months ago, thus proving the former war correspondent's idea of utopia is perpetual war.

May 13

West Virginia primary (Clinton)

May 14

Edwards endorses Obama

May 20

Oregon primary (Obama)
Kentucky primary (Clinton)

May 31

Democratic rules committee decides in Washington to give Florida and Michigan half votes at convention

Fantasy Island

There was plenty of grist for the pundit mill in the events leading up to this messy conclusion. Down almost 200 delegates, with only three contests left to go, Clinton decided to focus her attention in the last week on Puerto Rico. Puerto Ricans cannot vote in November, but will have 55 delegates at the convention. She went there not looking for a high delegate count, but a high voter turnout that would bolster her claim to be the most popular contender.

Her campaign had devolved to a series of ifs. If she could claim she won significantly more popular votes in the Democratic contests than Obama . . . if the Democratic rules committee accepted the results of the contested Florida and Michigan primaries as legitimate . . . if party regulars could be convinced she ran better than Obama in key swing states like Ohio, Pennsylvania and West Virginia, then she could make the case to the convention that she deserved the nomination.

Puerto Rico was the first rail in a three-rail bank shot she needed to sink the eight ball for a final victory. (One staffer called it her Fantasy Island.) She won, and by a wide margin (68 to 32 percent), but only 20 percent of voters turned out (384,000 instead of the 700,000 — 900,000 Clinton wanted) so it did little to bolster her popular vote claim.

Split The Baby

That wobbly win was overshadowed by a clear loss when the 30 members of the Democratic Rules and Bylaws committee met in Washington, D.C. last weekend to resolve the Florida and Michigan dispute.

Thirteen members of the committee were committed Clinton supporters. Only eight had declared their allegiance to Obama. But Clinton was asking a lot of them all — to put aside penalties they themselves had imposed on the states for jumping their primary dates ahead of Super Tuesday, effectively changing the rules in the middle of the game to undercut Obama's lead.

At stake were the 368 delegates Florida and Michigan would have sent under normal circumstances to the Denver convention. Last fall (eons ago, it seems) the Democratic National Committee voted overwhelmingly to strip Florida and Michigan of their delegates if they did not move back their primary dates. In a show of unity, all the Democratic candidates, including Clinton, pledged not to campaign there. In Michigan, Obama and the other candidates

June 1

Puerto Rican primary (Clinton)

June 1

Obama has spent total of $244 million to date on 2008 race, Clinton spent $225 million, McCain spent $84 million

June 3

Montana primary (Obama)
South Dakota primary (Clinton)

Obama claims nomination

Clinton makes "no decision"

(except Clinton and Mike Gravel) went so far as to take their names of the ballots.

But Florida and Michigan went ahead anyway. Nearly 1.7 million Democrats went to the polls in Florida. They gave Clinton 50 percent of their votes, Obama 33 percent, and John Edwards 14 percent. In Michigan, just over 600,000 Democrats voted. Fifty-five percent voted for Clinton and 40 percent marked "uncommitted" — a last ditch option put on the ballot by Obama forces to blunt Clinton's uncontested status.

For Clinton to make her case that she won the popular voting, those 2.3 million votes had to be added in; more important, to have any chance of winning on the convention floor, she needed every one of the delegates they represented.

Clinton's chances of winning in the rules committee were slim. Two days before the meeting, the committee's legal staff advised that the minimum penalty required was splitting the delegation votes in half.

On Friday night, the committee members met privately for a long and libatious dinner that lasted until 2 AM. Don Fowler, the former national party chairman from South Carolina, and Harold Ickes, a battle-hardened party insider renown for his willingness to argue over the consistency of butter, used the occasion to lobby for Clinton's cause. Ickes argued that a "fair reflection" of voter intent required counting all the delegates. Fowler more judiciously probed and prodded for points of compromise.

When the committee convened in public Saturday morning, three hours were set aside for Florida and Michigan to make their cases. Politicians being politicians, this stretched to five with no sign of abating. The committee adjourned for another private lunch. While Clinton supporters chanted in the hallways, lunch lingered on for three more hours and cable news commentators began to smell a deal.

When it returned to a public session, the committee took all of 20 minutes to conclude the proceedings. Clinton advocates were given a chance to say their piece. Then the votes were taken:

A motion to seat the full Florida delegation was defeated (15 to 12.) A motion to seat the Floria delegation with a half-vote for each was passed (unanimously.) And a motion to "split the baby" in Michigan based on a compromise proposed by the Michigan Democratic Party was offered. It called for cutting the delegation size in half, giving all the "uncommitted" votes to delegates approved by Obama, and compensating Obama for the 30,000 Obama write-in votes Michigan officials never counted by taking away four delegates from Clinton and giving them to Obama. (This passed 19-8.)

The net-net of it all was a re-calibration of the majority needed to win nomination from 2,026 to 2,118 and a 25.5-delegate gain for Clinton — that still left her 175.5 delegates behind Obama.

Clinton's last best hope to reverse the Obama tide was over.

June 6

Oil surges $11 to $138 a barrel record

June 7

Clinton suspends campaign, endorses Obama

June 8

USA Today/ Gallup poll

Obama 47%
McCain 43%

The 3 AM Phone Call

Clinton's primary campaign relied heavily on a TV commercial touting her readiness to answer that 3 AM phone call to the White House requiring an instant response to another presidential crisis. If you think of the last day of this campaign as 3 AM, you might need to rethink whether you want Hillary Clinton there to answer it.

After Puerto Rico, the lone remaining primaries were in South Dakota and Montana. For two days, Bill and Hillary Clinton careened around those states like drunken sailors on their last shore leave knowing the best they could hope for was picking up another delegate or two. (Clinton wound up gaining one.)

Clinton advisors who saw the endgame coming tiptoed around what she would do next. They urged the media to give her time to adjust to the political realities. The inner circle of advisors supporting her desire to soldier on shrunk to Ickes, husband Bill and Terry McAuliffe, her chief fundraiser and hopelessly optimistic cheerleader.

Meanwhile the Obama campaign apparatus shifted into high gear to pull in the last superdelegates needed to take them over the finish line. Watching it operate was like watching a fine-tuned Maserati click off practice laps on a dry track.

When Election Day dawned, Obama was 41 delegates short of the 2,118 needed to win. Twenty-four hours later, he was 34 delegates ahead. Only 15 of those came out of the South Dakota and Montana voting. The other 60 were superdelegates who first trickled, then flocked into his corner.

Clinton too was calling around to the supers on Election Day so it should have come as no surprise that her support was waning. At 3 o'clock, CNN reported Obama had closed the gap to 27 delegates. By 5 o'clock, it was down to 12. By 6 o'clock, CNN reported Obama was only six delegates short of the magic number. Any combination of votes in Montana or South Dakota would put him over.

In the middle of this frenzy, at 3:28 PM, the *Associated Press* reported that Clinton told her New York Democratic congressional colleagues in a conference call that if Obama offered her the vice-presidency spot on the ticket, she would consider taking it.

The cable news channels crackled with punditry on the possibilities. Superdelegates appearing on air to announce their choice were pressed to endorse a combo ticket. If Clinton wanted the VP spot, she had two-and-a-half hours to prepare a speech that would open the door.

And what did she do? She gave a speech that might have been the best defense of her candidacy she has ever offered. Unfortunately, it was the wrong speech at the wrong time. She not only misjudged the moment, she failed to see her own place in it. At a moment that called for graciousness, she was defiant. When the time came to let go, she held on.

A Nightmare Scenario

What presidential candidate in his right mind would want to share center stage with a running mate intent on one-upping him? A running mate who defends hanging on to the bitter end by conjuring up images of Bobby Kennedy in California (where he was assassinated) and stakes her claim to a position on the ticket on her appeal to uneducated white voters who will never vote for Obama anyway?

Clinton's speech in New York Tuesday night was anything but a job application. She outlined all the reasons she thinks she is a better candidate and, in case she missed any, invited listeners to go to her website to offer their own.

David Gergen, a White House counselor to Presidents Nixon, Ford, Reagan and Clinton, likened it to Nixon's Checkers speech in 1952 — a last gasp appeal to the public to save her candidacy.

As to the chances Clinton's speech improved her vice presidential prospects: "It just re-enforces the notion she is difficult to deal with," Gergen scoffed.

"She's saying 'I'm leading 18 million people and you're going to have to deal with me to reach them.'"

"It's like the Clintons are living in a parallel universe," said an incredulous Gloria Borger.

"The New York delegation is with her to the end, but we thought the end was the end," added a frustrated Rep. Charles Rangell (D-NY). "So we're going to have to get some direction from her (about what's going on)."

Clinton's speech highlighted the fact Bill and Hillary Clinton are their own show, poorly suited to play second fiddle to anyone. They came to power in 1992 as party outsiders, took over the party apparatus during Clinton's White House years, and even after four years out of power, flooded John Kerry's 2004 campaign with advisors and advice on what he was doing wrong. Barack Obama needs Hillary Clinton on the ticket like he needs a Jeremiah Wright Comeback Tour.

One reason Clinton loyalists say Obama should put Clinton on the ticket is to heal the breach she has created between Obama and her base of white women, senior citizens and blue-collar voters. If recent exit polls are to be believed, as many as half of her supporters say they will abstain or vote for McCain if Clinton is not the Democratic candidate. These primary passions tend to disappear, however, when Republicans and Democrats begin to look at their own self-interest in the fall. When talk of the dream ticket fades (and the longer Clinton persists in proclaiming her superiority, the sooner it will,) Obama knows he has plenty of worthy alternatives.

My suggestion would be that Obama recruit Al Gore for another go-round. Why not? Gore already knows where the fuse box is in the vice-president's residence; and he's already won the presidency once. He could make the environmental policy his personal dominion and, except for the light lifting required to preside over the Senate and cast tie-breaking votes, devote himself to stopping global warming and not just lecturing about.

Another game-changing option would be New York Mayor Michael Bloomberg, who has been courted already by both parties. If Obama is concerned about swing states, there's Ohio Gov. Ted Strickland, a Clinton supporter. If he wants to balance the ticket with a woman (from a swing state), he might try Missouri Sen. Claire McCaskill.

His mission right now is to find a running mate who complements the campaign he ran, someone who shares his vision and whom he can rely on to help execute it. No one is further from that description than Hillary Clinton. But that decision comes further down the road.

Stay tuned.

PART TWO

Lipstick On A Pig

The Lay of The Land

July 12, 2008

"This is not the end, nor even the beginning of the end, but it is, finally, the end of the beginning."

– Winston Churchill

VACATION IS OVER.

Hillary Clinton went to Martha's Vineyard to drown her sorrows. Barack Obama flew to Montana to get in touch with his inner cowboy. And John McCain went off hunting drug smugglers in Columbia while Karl Rove re-organized his campaign staff around Steve Schmidt and other veterans from President Bush's 2004 re-election team.

Before we get too excited about this summer simmer leading up to the fall campaign it is wise to remember that the last time we went to the polls to elect a president, America was a 47-47 nation.

Forty-seven percent of the 122 million people who cast presidential ballots in 2004 favored the Republican candidate George Bush; 47 percent favored Democrat John

June 13

Tim Russert dies

June 17

Washington Post/ ABC poll

Obama 48 %
McCain 42 %

June 19

Obama opts out of public financing in fall election.

June 25

Obama unveils '50-state strategy' to hold 4 blue states, go after 14 red states from 2004 election.

Kerry; and six percent walked into the polls claiming they were still undecided. That division was roughly the same four years earlier in 2000 and there is no reason to think it will change dramatically this election year.

Presidential campaigns do not, as a rule, change many minds. They simply lead to changing presidents. Far more important than the philosophy of the candidates is the topography of the political landscape. A flare-up of domestic terrorism, a deepening economic depression or a storm of violence in Iraq are more likely to influence the outcome of this election than any candidate's position on health care, global warming, fair trade pacts or illegal immigration.

Barack Obama has successfully defined this year as a change election, although that's not saying much. It's easy enough to throw the bums out of Washington since the bum-in-chief, President Bush, is leaving anyway. The task for Obama and John McCain is to define what kind of "change" each will bring if he is elected. Much of what is soon to transpire will go toward sharpening the distinctions between their two visions of the future.

This begins over the summer with a kind of pin the tail on the donkey game. Obama will take every opportunity to emphasize that John McCain is running for George Bush's third term. McCain, in turn, will refer to Obama as a typical tax and spend liberal Democrat. And the vast preponderance of voters — some experts put that at around 90 percent, split about evenly — will need to hear little more to vote as they always do, against the other guy.

This means the next billion dollars spent on this presidential race will go toward convincing the other ten percent, and it will be spent three ways:

1) Mobilize the Base.

If most voters already have made up their minds about whom they support, then the key for both candidates is to get those voters to the polls. Registration drives, Get Out The Vote (GOTV) operations, Rock the Vote concerts (for Democrats) and faith-based initiatives (for Republicans) are all ways to motivate your natural constituencies.

Finding the names and addresses of individuals in those constituencies and getting them to the polls has become a computerized art form. Both parties now maintain huge databases linked to sophisticated consumer marketing research that identifies the traits of each candidate's potential supporters (latte-drinking, Volvo-driving, Birkenstock-wearing liberals being the most famous category). One company has identified as many as 150 consumer preferences that can, in combination, predict a voter's political preference.

In more ways than we probably want to acknowledge, the party that has mastered this new political art form stands the best chance of winning in November.

June 26

Gallup Daily Tracking Poll

Obama 44 %
McCain 44 %

2) Capture the Swing Voters.

In 2002, a young pollster working in President Bush's political office came to a remarkable conclusion. Matt Dowd was hired by Karl Rove to analyze the results of the 1996 and 2000 election. The more he studied the returns, the more he came to believe the so-called "swing voters" both sides tried so hard to woo amounted to only about seven percent of the electorate.

July 11

Oil prices peak at $147 per barrel

Instead of fighting over this small sliver, he suggested to Rove that Bush devote more energy to turning out his party base. That became the cornerstone of Rove's winning strategy in the 2004 election.

While Democrats concentrated on registering more than two million (mostly young) new voters, Rove turned out four million more Republicans by mining conservative strongholds in churches, rural communities and the exurbs outside major cities.

Ironically, the political landscape this year is considerably different. Swing voters are back in vogue. One reason is that neither McCain nor Obama are traditional party candidates. After a 20-year career as a maverick, McCain does not have a dyed-in-the-wool conservative base to turn to; and Obama, as Hillary Clinton made clear, cannot necessarily count on the blue collar, white vote that makes up a key component in the traditional Democratic coalition.

Because both ran well in the primaries among so-called independents, both are likely to target people still sitting on the fence in the fall.

3) Win the Battleground States

The red state–blue state divide in America is real despite what Obama told the Democratic convention in 2004. California and New York are not going to vote Republican this year. Kentucky, Utah, Texas, Oklahoma, Wyoming, West Virginia, South Carolina, Mississippi and Alabama are not going to go Democratic.

Pollsters are fond of breaking down candidate support by age, race, religion and gender. It's worth reminding ourselves, however, that presidents are not chosen by any of these groups, or even the popular vote total. The are chosen in the Electoral College on a state-by-state basis so both sides are once again concentrating their efforts on winning certain "battleground" states.

In 2004, there were 16 of these. Obama's strategists are hoping to expand the battlefield to 18. McCain strategists also have 18 target states in mind (though not all the same ones) so only 20 states, at most, are likely to see any significant influx of TV spending, direct mail or door-to-door campaigning.

At the end of June, Obama's campaign manager David Plouffe gave the Democratic National Committee a Powerpoint preview of how Obama intended to win those 18 states. His targets are Alaska, Colorado, Georgia, Indiana, Michigan, Iowa, Missouri, Montana, Florida, Nevada, New Hampshire, New Mexico, North Carolina, North Dakota, Ohio, Pennsylvania, Wisconsin and Virginia. All but Michigan, Pennsylvania, New Hampshire and Wisconsin went Republican in 2004.

According to Plouffe's analysis, if Democrats can increase voter turnout ten percent among just the African-American and young voters in those states, Obama has a fighting chance of taking them all. (In fact, if Obama holds on to all the states Kerry won in 2004, he only has to win Florida or Ohio to get the 270 electoral votes he needs to win.)

If, on the other hand, McCain holds on in Florida, Ohio, Georgia, North Carolina, Indiana and Missouri — and Republicans can pick up Michigan or Pennsylvania (both primary states Obama did poorly in) — Obama could win most of the other 18 target states and still lose.

One danger McCain faces this year (that Bush did not in 2004) is the presence in the race of former Georgia Congressman Bob Barr as the Libertarian Party candidate. If Barr can mobilize the forces that backed Ron Paul in the primaries, he might draw away as much as three to six percent of the Republican vote in Georgia, Alaska, New Hampshire, Michigan and Pennsylvania, thus throwing a monkey wrench into McCain's fall strategy.

Another factor that makes this election different from all the others is the extraordinary media coverage, not just in the mainstream media but in all the new forms the Internet has made possible. The speed with which issues arise and are disseminated around the news outlets has given this campaign an urgency unlike any before. *New York Times* columnist Frank Rich calls it "a 24/7 news culture that inflates any passing tit for tat into a war of the worlds."

Last week, it was Gen. Wesley Clark questioning McCain's military experience at the command level and McCain operatives jumping on Obama for "flip-flopping" on his Iraq pullout plan. In both cases, a statement in the morning was countered by instant Internet press releases, telephone press conference calls, clarifying press releases, non-stop analysis by "political strategists" on CNN's Situation Room and, ultimately, remorse the next day by news reporters who recognized they might have over-reacted. Expect more pseudo-news over the summer.

And watch the 527's — those nefarious independent political action committees on the fringes of both campaigns. They've been relatively silent so far, but the success of The Swift Boat Veterans for Truth in torpedoing John Kerry's 2004 presidential bid hangs out there like a

challenge to other well-funded groups to have an even greater impact this year.

Remember, when you can't hear the bats, that's when you know the bats are coming.

Let the games begin.

Campaign by Email

August 8, 2008

THE SUMMER DOLDRUMS **have done nothing to slow the pace of the presidential campaign this year.** Barack Obama in Europe and John McCain in town hall meetings across America churn the butter of politics as if a day without their face on the front page of a newspaper would sink their image to the bottom of the barrel.

The constant drumbeat of the campaign is especially noticeable in the email of the reporters covering the race. I opened my email box one day and found 24 missives from the two campaigns. These included not only the schedules for the candidates, but invitations to call in to telephone press conferences by surrogates, instant responses from one campaign to what the other's surrogate said, even a response to the response by the offending party.

Much has been made of how the Internet this year has turned into a powerhouse of political fundraising and field organization. Little is mentioned in the press about how the campaigns are using email to get to reporters, and how that is fundamentally changing the nature of the coverage.

The telephone press conference is a prime example. Almost every morning, at least one campaign will send out an email announcing that, for instance, Gen. Wesley Clark, will be holding a telephone press "avail" at 1 PM (EST). Reporters are invited to call an 800 number and provided an access code to listen in on the call. After Clark's brief opening remarks, they can then press a button, identify themselves and ask a question.

The conference calls draw a regular array of the top campaign reporters, as well as any blogger, radio talk show host, TV producer or hanger-on who gets the email. Both campaigns are guarded about how many people dial in. An Obama spokesman says the calls typically draw about 100 listeners. His counterpart in the McCain press office says it can be upwards of 500. That's twice the size of the entire accredited White House press corps.

The daily conference calls are a good indicator of what campaign story will appear that night on the evening network news. NBC's Andrea Mitchell and ABC's Jake Tapper are serial callers. On more than one occasion, I've

July 19

Obama begins 7-day trip to Afghanistan, Iraq, Israel and Europe

July 24

Obama speaks to 200,000 in Berlin; McCain visits former President George H. W. Bush in Kennebunkport

July 31

McCain releases "Celebrity Ad" comparing Obama to Britney Spears and Paris Hilton listened to Mitchell weave together a story on charges flying back and forth between the opposing camps based largely on quotes from these calls.

The very notion that there are Obama and McCain "camps" is fostered by the way the campaigns run their press operations. McCain's national press office is in Arlington, Virginia, with 11 regional press spokesmen scattered around the country. The size of the staff, the number of people on the press email lists (there are many lists), even who handles what tasks is a secret. "We consider that all a part of our campaign strategy," Wendy Riemann, my press representative in Illinois, told me. All communications with reporters come under the single email account press@mccainpress.com.

Obama's press office in Chicago is only slightly more forthcoming. I tried on nearly a dozen occasions, directly and through friends in the campaign, to arrange a personal interview with one of the spokesmen there, but I was told the office is closed to the press. (At Obama's recent speech to the Journalists of Color in Chicago, I asked the press advanceman, Grant Campbell, if he could take me down after the event. "Are you kidding? Even I have trouble getting in," he said.)

Fortunately, the Obama campaign sent out a press release last month announcing changes in its press office line-up. Robert Gibbs, his longtime advisor, was stepping up to be senior communications strategist. Bill Burton, the traveling press secretary, would become national press secretary and Dan Pfeiffer, former deputy communications director, would become the communications director. In all, the release listed 20 other key aides stepping into new roles in press management. The most curious appointments

August 8

John Edwards admits affair with campaign videographer

August 11

Democratic Convention schedule shows 300 parties planned

August 16

McCain and Obama appear at Rick Warren church forum

August 23

Obama announces Joe Biden as VP pick in text message to supporters

were Tommy Vietor and Hari Sevugan to handle rapid response.

The import of these changes became apparent in the next few weeks as emails started arriving in my box with the names of individual senders attached. If the email discusses a high level meeting between Obama and a foreign dignitary, it comes from rgibbs@barackobama.com. If it deals more with Obama's theme of the day, it carries the name of bburton. Copies of speeches or position papers come from nshapiro. Responses to McCain appearances or tips on favorable news articles in the papers come from tvietor or hsevugan.

Of all my new Obama pen pals, Vietor is by far the most entertaining. He mans the Gatling gun on the parapet of the Obama camp, and he's not averse to firing off four or five bursts of bullets every day.

"White House Accidentally E-Mails to Reporters Story That Maliki Supports Obama Iraq Withdrawal Plan," Vietor wrote on July 19, calling attention to an article in the German magazine *Der Spiegel.*

"John McCain is an honorable man who is running an increasingly dishonorable campaign," he wrote on July 26 after McCain released an ad taking a dig at Obama for going to the gym instead of visiting the troops.

"As some might say, 'Oops! He did it again,'" Vietor wrote on July 29 in response to McCain's ad comparing Obama to Paris Hilton and Britney Spears. "Even by the elastic standards of political ads, this is more than a stretch. It's baloney. It's also a marker on the path toward the kind of simplistic, counterproductive demonizing that many expect will poison the fall campaign."

Vietor's most famous email didn't come during this campaign but back in 2005 when, as Obama's Senate press secretary, he issued a press release praising the U.S. Department of Energy for giving $337 million to the O'Hare airport expansion.

"Going out on a limb as always, I see," Rich Miller, of *Capitol Fax*, chided him in an email.

"We are also pro-puppy, for the record," Vietor shot back.

"Does that mean he's anti-kitten?" Miller asked.

"No comment," Vietor replied.

Miller turned the exchange into a mock news story claiming "A top aide to U.S. Sen Barack Obama refused to confirm or deny that the popular freshman senator despises kittens" and the full exchange, like everything these days, lives on in the Internet archive of the *Illinois Times.*

Vietor and Sevugan, both in their 20's, share space in Obama's open office campaign headquarters, and there is a kind of "can you top this?" tone to their rapid response. Sevugan loads his emails up with quotes and congressional voting records. Vietor favors the found fact from the oddest places.

When McCain supporters in Michigan handed out tire gauges to mock Obama's energy conservation proposals, Vietor quickly sent out links to a NASCAR web site and a U.S. Department of Energy "Money Saving Tips" column claiming proper tire pressure can save 3.3% in fuel costs. Within hours, he'd also drummed up quotes from Gov. Arnold Schwarzenegger and Gov. Charlie Crist, both McCain supporters, urging the same conservation measure.

Although the McCain campaign also has a rapid response team, it can't keep up in volume or breadth of coverage. A 30-second McCain TV spot released yesterday criticizing Obama as anti-family drew an 8-page rebuttal (with 23 news source citations and six Congressional votes) from the Obama camp. Moments later, Vietor piled on with a quote from McCain's potential running mate Minnesota Governor Tim Pawlenty that he unearthed from a GOPAC meeting the same day: "Say what you will about Barack Obama, people gravitate when you have something positive to say...People want to follow hopeful, optimistic, civil, decent leaders. They don't want to follow some negative, scornful person."

Much of what passes back and forth between the campaigns will have little impact on real voters; but because it is so widespread, there is no telling what items will catch on, or where. A juicy tidbit highlighting an opponent's hypocrisy can roil the blogosphere for the day or feed the guest strategists on the afternoon cable news shows for a week.

If all voters had to go by this election year were the pronouncements coming out of the campaign press offices, it would paint a bleak picture of two petty politicians picking at each other's scabs . . . which, come to think of it, is what the campaign looks like this week.

The Democratic Convention: I'm Going In

August 22, 2008

OKAY, I'M GOING in . . . and we'll just see what there is to see.

I'm still working on this pesky credentials problem. You might think that, as chief political correspondent of *The Week Behind*, a press pass would be a snap. Alas, I think they are on to me.

The good news is that the Democrats have cleared out the riff raff from around the Pepsi Center so delegates can jog unmolested along the Platte River. To keep them otherwise occupied, the city of Denver has installed big screen TVs in various homeless shelters so, worst case, I can watch the Democratic convention with the homeless.

But I'm hoping to do better than that.

The Phantom Beast

I'll be driving around Denver in this Phantom Beast of a truck, a Ford F-150 pick-up, thrust upon me by the exigency

August 24 – 29

Democratic Convention in Denver

of an American economy spinning out of control. Back in May, when I went to rent a car, gas was running $4.50 a gallon. Every politician with a toe still left in the presidential pool had a plan to curb our dependence on foreign oil, and 180,000 of these gas guzzlers were sitting unsold on the car lots of America.

For 17 years in a row, the F-150 truck had been the best selling vehicle in America, of any kind. Cars, trucks, SUV's, you name it. The F-150 outsold them all. Why? Because this baby is the workhorse of the American economy. Its 350 horsepower, 5.4 litre V-8 engine has a tow capacity of five tons and a cargo hold capable of carrying 3,000 pounds. It comes standard with dual reinforced side rails, a single overhead cam, telescoping mirrors — and an insulated tool chest behind the cab capable of holding 60 pounds of beer.

Seven times, it has been named *Motor Trends*' Truck of the Year. Now Ford can't give them away. So when the rental car company offered me a two-door Chevy Aveo for $468 a week or an F-150 for $143 less, I jumped on it. Does that come with the optional rear window gun rack?

Global Warming Brigade, Sign Me Up!

I know, my choice of vehicles won't go over big with the environmental crowd, and the environment is very much on the minds of Democratic conventioneers this year. For the first time in history, the Democrats will have an official "Director of Greening." She is one Andrea Robinson, who trained for the position by playing Nurse Nancy opposite Billy Rae Cyrus in the TV series "Doc."

Ms. Robinson comes to the Democrats after a stint managing garbage cans at Giants Stadium and Shanghai for Al Gore's 2007 Live Earth concerts, and she has issued guidelines this year governing everything from the biodegradable quality of the convention balloons to the color of the food on the party tables. At least three of the following colors: red, green, yellow, blue/purple and white (garnishes not included) must be used on the theory colorful food is more vibrant.

To meet her goal of recycling 85 percent of the convention waste materials, she's gathered a staff of 900 volunteers to police the trash bins and asked contractors working on the convention stage to emphasize reusable building materials in the construction.

Robinson has also established a contest among the state delegations to see who can reduce their carbon footprint the most, promising the winner seats closer to the convention stage, and here's where I think I might be of some assistance.

So far only three states have taken up the challenge: California, Vermont and Nevada. Nevada seems to have the inside track since the stage is being built there (using soy-based paints and no fiberglass or Styrofoam) and will be trucked into Denver on vehicles using only bio-diesel fuel.

But I'm thinking of calling up the Indiana delegation and suggesting we go after the prize together. I'll rent a flatbed trailer and drive the whole delegation back and forth to the convention on less than a gallon of gas a day (provided their hotel is inside a seven mile radius of the Pepsi Center.) We'll tie biodegradable balloons to the tailgate, put the beer on ice, use the tool chest for our empties, and serve complimentary corn chips with jalapeno and guacamole (green, red and yellow) along the way.

Hell, we may never make it out of the parking out. We'll just ask for a show of hands at the roll call and text message in the results. And when we're finished, we'll drive over to the recycling center ourselves to drop off the cans. With scrap aluminum going for 66 cents a pound, we'll more than cover the cost.

Why I'm Going

Why me and the Phantom Beast are really going to Denver is to remind the Democrats there are more important things than whether the balloons are biodegradable.

In 2005, the heyday of the F-150, Ford sold nearly one million small trucks. 86,200 people made their living working on the Ford assembly lines that cranked them out. Today, that number is down to 56,500. If you ripple those 30,000 lost jobs at Ford through all the other companies that made parts or supplied services to Ford, it's a pretty good indicator of what's happening in America.

The alleged villain in this downturn is the high price of gasoline. The F-150 gets on average 14 to 20 miles per gallon (compared with the compact cars that now advertise 32 mpg) and F-150 sales are down 18% so far this year. The slump, however, is only partially due to soaring oil prices.

The more critical factor is that American consumers now fear our economy is going to hell in a handbasket and are pulling in the purse strings. Overall car sales in America, regardless of mileage, are down 11 percent this year, unemployment is up to 5.7 percent — a four year high — and wholesale prices in July jumped almost 10 percent over a year ago.

Our confidence that we will have a good job, affordable health care, money to educate our children and, yes, buy a new car every once in a while is at the lowest point in 20 years. Faith in the ability of our leaders in Washington to find solutions to these problems is even lower. As James Carville famously advised another Democratic candidate 16 years ago, Barack Obama should never forget, "It's the economy, stupid!"

Not many of those attending the Democratic convention this year are likely to be personally affected by this. The salaries of politicians and lobbyists are particularly resistant to economic recessions; and when the boss comes around to lay you off, your first instinct isn't to say "Hey,

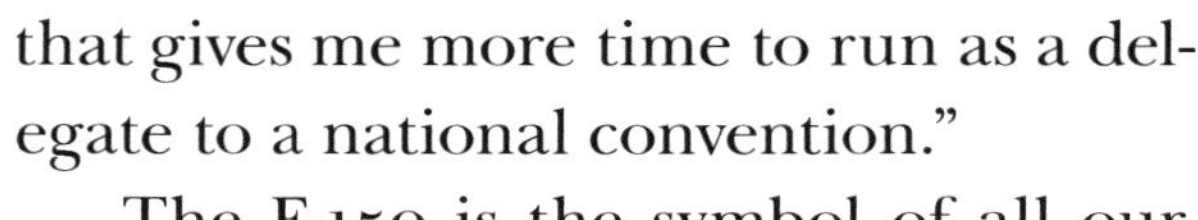

that gives me more time to run as a delegate to a national convention."

The F-150 is the symbol of all our frustration. It's a working man's truck. We use it to take hay bales from the feed store back to the farm, old refrigerators to the garbage dump and all our worldly belongings to the next place when we get foreclosed on the last.

It's a beautiful example of American ingenuity. It may get half the gas mileage of a Prius, but it's capable of doing four times the work. And that's all American workers are asking, a chance to work.

So if you're out in Denver next week, look for an F-150 with Obama "Hope" posters on the doors. That'll be me and the Phantom Beast laying down skid marks all over the buffet tables.

Southwick

August 24, 2008

In '69, I was twenty-one and I called the road my own
I don't know when that road turned onto the road I'm on
Running on empty — running blind
Running into the sun but I'm running behind
–Jackson Browne

I'M STAYING IN Denver with Southwick, an old friend from college who is loosely affiliated with the host committee. After he left college, Southwick went to Washington to make his way up the ladder of good government. He rose, in fact, high enough to become press secretary to Senator Ted Kennedy during his 1980 presidential campaign against Jimmy Carter.

I was living at the time on Webster Street in Chicago in a storefront with a ping-pong table, a loft bed and a killer stereo system. It was about a week before the Illinois primary, a contest Kennedy had locked up with the endorsement of Chicago Mayor Jane Bryne, when my doorbell rang.

Through the peephole, I could see Southwick standing outside. He was wearing a crumpled suit, his tie stripped off, carrying all his worldly belongings in a satchel. He asked if he could crash at my place.

"For how long?" I asked.

"For the rest of my life," he said.

And that's pretty much what he did that night, tossing his bag on the floor, crawling into the loft bed and cranking up Jackson Browne's "Running on Empty" in an endless loop on the stereo.

The next day his tale of treachery along the campaign trail began to unfold. Kennedy's early primary fortunes had not gone as hoped. Mediating the conflicting advice Kennedy was getting, dodging reporter questions, all the while moving city to city in a hopeless cause, was a little more than Southwick signed on for.

His brain was fried. He couldn't remember where he'd slept the night before, who he had talked to, or the last time he called his wife. (This was before cell phones.) The exhausting schedule put a strain on his relations with Kennedy, and on his marriage. In the end, the floundering campaign was handed over to "wiser" heads and Southwick was shipped off to Illinois where his main job was riding the press bus collecting lunch money from the reporters.

Every morning, he'd leave at the crack of dawn dressed like a K Street lobbyist. Every night, he'd return looking like he'd just finished a hard day on the floor of the Penney's menswear department. He'd strip off his tie, climb under the covers — and on came Jackson Browne.

When the primary was over, the last I saw of Southwick he was sitting on a Greyhound bus headed west. "Working at McDonalds has to be more steady employment than this," he said. He resigned from the campaign and never returned to Washington.

Let this be a cautionary tale to all you bright young campaign workers riding along on the Obama bandwagon: Politics can be an exhilarating ride when you're on top — and a cruel ditch of sewage water filled with viperous colleagues when you are not.

Once Southwick reached Denver, he caught on as editor of a little trade magazine that covered the cable TV industry. As cable television emerged from a community antenna system into a media powerhouse, he moved from being a reporter of the business to a participant, joining John Malone's Starz as senior vice president of corporate communications and government relations.

At the convention this year, Southwick will be presiding over The Starz Green Room, a reception area inside the security perimeter of the Pepsi Center. They will be showing old political films and holding panel discussions with a good number of the Hollywood celebrities attending the convention. Ben Affleck, Daryl Hannah, Arianna Huffington, Will.i.am, Josh Brolin and Michael Moore have all signed on. I'll be hanging my hat there as well. Since all any

reporter really needs these days is a cell phone and a laptop, there's no need for *The Week Behind* to book a suite in the media center (like anyone offered).

I've got "The Best of Jackson Browne" loaded into the CD-player and I'm headed out now to Southwick's place in the Denver foothills for a welcome concert at the Red Rocks Amphitheatre.

But first, I have to make a little pit stop downtown to see how we're coming on the credentials front. It's not that I'm worried, but it's better to get these things out of the way before trouble sets in.

Waiting on Buckman

August 25, 2008

I'm running down the road trying to loosen my load
Seven women on my mind
Four that want to own me, two that want to stone me,
One says she's a friend of mine
Take it easy, take it easy . . .
Don't let the sound of your own wheels drive you crazy.
– Jackson Browne

WHEN I ARRIVE, DOWNTOWN DENVER IS A TRAFFIC NIGHTMARE. Gridlock on all the main streets. Buses lined up wall-to-wall near the key venues. Every time one tries to turn, it cantilevers across the intersection blocking every lane. Sandwiched in between the buses are 500 taxis Denver has imported for the convention, not to mention all the gawkers in SUV's who came in from the suburbs to see what Democrats look like.

Meanwhile, on every street corner, there are eight or ten police in spanking-new riot gear: black jump suits with plastic handcuffs Velcro-ed to their legs and ever-so-sporty, bulbous riot helmets with flipped up plastic face shields on their heads that make them look like Ninja Turtles.

The federal government this year gave Denver $50 million for convention security and it's pretty clear where it all went — into the uniforms. You'd think, somewhere in all that training, they'd have taught some of these cops how to direct traffic. But none of the cops lifts a finger to unsnarl the mess.

I make my way to the Marriott where the Illinois delegation is staying. I'm there to meet Richard Buckman, the elusive political operative who guided me through the last Democratic convention in Boston. Through the spring and summer, Buckman has been regaling me with text messages from his BlackBerry on the good times we are going to have in Denver.

"Can take care of all your convention needs with floor and press passes this year my friend! :)" he texted last March.

"So bro, it's all my guy Obama tonight," he texted on June 3 when

Obama wrapped up the nomination. "Ready for Denver???? Got you covered."

I'm sitting in the lobby of the Marriott. A life-size cardboard cutout of Barack is standing next to me, but there's no sign of Buckman. I pull out my flip phone (the old postage stamp kind) and tap out my own little text message to Buckman: "I'm here. Where r u?"

Even as I send it off, I know something is amiss. The last round of text messages from Buckman carried an ominous tone. "Hey, bro . . . you wouldn't happen to have $5K lying around. Will get it back to you in a few days," he wrote in July. Then in August, "I know I haven't updated you but I will in Denver . . . struggling until then bro."

Buckman is a rogue, no doubt about that, but a charming rogue nonetheless. The few hundred dollars I could spare, I wired to him after his last entreaty, knowing I would never see it again. Somehow, I still think he will show up here at the last minute, just as he did in Boston, dangling a string of party invitations around his neck.

But it never hurts to have a Plan B. I call my friend Scrounger back in Chicago, a woman so powerful one dare not speak her name, and allow I might need a little help. "So what do you need? Floor pass? Press pass? Hall pass? How many?" is all she asks.

No sooner had I hung up than my phone rings with another text message — from Buckman: "Got your message. Will buzz you back in a bit."

That was three hours ago. No call. No further contact. If you are waiting for a call on your cell phone, it really doesn't matter where you are when the phone doesn't ring.

So I decide to take a little walk downtown to catch a few parties.

The big one is the Democratic National Committee Tribute to Hurricane Relief Organizations in the Colorado Convention Center. It's one of those free feeds the party puts on for delegates and guests who haven't been invited to any of the good parties, and about 3,000 people show up.

I look around hoping to find Buckman working the room, vindication of my faith in him, but the crowd turned out to be mostly mooches, T-shirt salesmen and media types (and cops sitting around in riot gear). Even New Orleans Mayor Ray Nagin, whose city is the chief beneficiary of this shindig, makes only a 20-minute cameo appearance before hustling off to the next affair.

It was not an auspicious start on the party front. But the next morning, there was another message on my cell phone. "Pick up your credentials at the Brown Palace at 3 PM. Have fun." Scrounger scores again.

The Lion Roars, The Pussycat Purrs

August 26, 2008

THERE WAS ALWAYS **a question whether Sen. Ted Kennedy** would speak Monday at the Democratic convention, always a question in the minds of everyone except Kennedy.

Once word passed that he had made it to Denver, there was no keeping the 76-year-old Senator away. Not a malignant brain tumor, not months of chemotherapy, not doctors afraid he might over-exert himself in the thin mountain air. This was, perhaps, the last time the lion would roar, and he knew it.

"I have come here tonight to stand with you to change America, to restore its future, to rise to our best ideals, and to elect Barack Obama president of the United States," he said.

"Teddy. . . Teddy . . . Teddy," the crowd roared back.

Kennedy is the youngest of three remarkable brothers — John, Bobby and Ted — but arguably the one who has had the greatest impact on our national government. In his 46 years in the Senate, he has revised our criminal justice code, expanded health care to millions and championed dozens of causes from early childhood education to better body armor for our troops in Iraq. Victory in the presidential arena was not to be his, but in the Senate, he has a record of accomplishment not seen since Daniel Webster.

Bob Shrum, his former speechwriter who went on to become a political consultant, told the *National Journal* that Kennedy took particular pleasure in the fact that what would never be his could now be Barack Obama's.

"For him, it is a joyful passing," Shrum said. "Before he was sick, he specifically said it's time for a new generation, and he said that Obama reminded him of his brother. Look, this is a powerful moment in the history of the party."

To mark that passing, Kennedy borrowed some phrases from speeches of old, notably his 1980 Democratic convention speech, and added some new.

"For me, this is a season of hope, new hope for a just and fair prosperity for the many, and not just for the few," he said. "And this is the cause of my life: new hope that we will break the old gridlock and guarantee that every

American — north, south, east, west, young, old — will have decent, quality health care as a fundamental right and not a privilege."

I stood near the front of the podium looking out at the crowd. The teleprompter stuttered forward to keep pace with Kennedy's rhythms. He missed a few lines, but replaced them on the fly with others even more powerful . . . and his own.

The last were vintage Kennedy: "This November, the torch will be passed again to a new generation of Americans. The work begins anew, hope rises again and the dream lives on."

Kennedy stepped back from the podium a minute as if catching his breath. The rising swell of the crowd response brought him forward again. Raw instinct told him what to do. He raised his hand in triumph and smiled while the band struck up "Still the One" and his wife Vicki led him from the stage.

Michelle's Moment

Michelle Obama's task Monday night was harder — to walk the line between the role of dutiful wife and competent professional without alienating the many staunch Hillary Clinton supporters in the audience or, alternatively, giving the Republicans a new target to go after.

In opening the convention with the story of Michelle, Obama's campaign strategists set the table for a week that will show America the Obamas are a family "just like us," or, more correctly, "so much like us they are who we would be if we were more like who we want to be."

With Kennedy's presence still in the hall, it was not hard (or unintended) to imagine the Obamas as the next Kennedys and an Obama White House as the next Camelot. Michelle's silky-smooth delivery of the lines about the values she and Barack grew up on: "you work hard for what you want in life," "your word is your bond," "you do what you say you're going to do," and "you treat people with dignity and respect" set the Obamas firmly in the center of mainstream America.

Couple that with the gauzy video narrated by her mother about the struggles Michelle's MS-stricken father went through as a city water worker putting his two children through college; her brother's teasing about her ability to memorize every episode of The Brady Bunch; and, finally, a long and personable story about her first date with Barack and his awkward attempt to woo her with an ice cream cone, and you have, in the ballpark of family values, a home run.

The Soft Sell

Besides introducing herself, Michelle had to introduce her husband, and she did it in the same even-toned spirit. She told of returning with him to a South Side neighborhood in Chicago where he had organized out-of-work steelworkers. "They were parents living paycheck to paycheck, grandparents trying to get by on a fixed income, men frustrated that they couldn't support their families after their jobs disappeared," she said, "ordinary folks, doing the best they could to build a good life."

On television, James Carville, the longtime Clinton advisor more comfortable these days as a TV commentator, derided Michelle's speech as a "wasted night." He wants the Democrats to go after McCain, and go after him hard, hitting at Republican weaknesses in foreign policy, taxation and economic policy. That is, perhaps, why Sen. Clinton is not the Democratic nominee this year.

The closer for Michelle's night in the limelight was a made-for-TV piece of trickery. After Michelle brought her two daughters, Malia, 10, and Sasha,7, to the stage, Barack himself suddenly appeared from Kansas City in a magic TV box previously hidden by the podium.

"How do you think mom did?" he asked them.

"I think she did good," Sasha said.

"I think so, too," Malia said.

"So do I," her father replied, then Malia added, "We love you, Daddy."

You may or may not want Obama to be president next year, but you'll never be embarrassed seeing his family in the White House.

Hillary Delivers

August 27, 2008

Fountain of sorrow, fountain of light
You've known that hollow sound
Of your own steps in flight
You've had to hide sometimes but now you're all right
And it's good to see your smiling face tonight.

–*Jackson Browne*

TUESDAY WAS A day of waiting. Waiting for the other woman in Barack Obama's life to speak. Waiting to see what Hillary Clinton would say.

With the Democratic convention now officially launched, delegates are starting to search for ways to fill the day between speeches. I made my usual stop at the Marriott this morning and found a handful of Illinois delegates massing for a "Bike for Change" ride through downtown Denver.

Up at the Brown Palace, the Democratic Senatorial Committee was hosting a breakfast for contributors of $30,000 or more; *The Nation* was feting its stable of writers at a luncheon for liberals; and the *Christian Science Monitor* was hosting a brunch/press conference featuring, of all people, Mitt Romney.

I caught up with Romney as he bounded up the stairs to ask what he was doing here. "In this day of 24-hour news cycles, people are talking about issues and they're not going to let another party get away with generalities," he told me. Then he told the same thing to ABC, the next reporter down the line, and later to all the cable news channels. Nobody ever said Romney can't stay on script.

Over at the Sheraton, Clinton was the star of the show at the Emily's List Gala. A few hours later, Michelle Obama made a similar star turn at Mayor Daley's reception for the Illinois delegation in the Denver Performing Arts Center. Clinton gave few hints on what her message of the night would be. Obama proved her speech Monday was no fluke, repeating all the key lines without a teleprompter and seamlessly spinning off into why she and Barack chose Chicago in particular to raise their family.

With little enthusiasm and not much interest, the cable news channels chattered through the afternoon about "ongoing negotiations" between the Clinton and Obama camps over how, exactly,

Clinton could get her roll call vote Wednesday without disrupting Obama's prime time show. In the *New York Times* this morning, Patrick Healy characterized the drama in Denver as three political dynasties, the Kennedys, the Obamas and the Clintons, trying to find a way to share the same stage.

Healy reported Senator Clinton was frustrated at the role she's been cast in. "And Mr. Clinton believes, viscerally, that the Obama camp framed him as a race-baiter." Healy's observations were based mainly on interviews with Clinton friends and advisors. The principals, however, were mum so what Hillary said Tuesday night would be, in the end, the final word.

Making My Way To The Hall

I made my way down to the Pepsi Center along the 16th Street mall, where the public trolley gives delegates free rides to the convention hall and protestors gather to plug their special causes. These included stopping government spying, bird porn, bullshit, global warming (by taxing meat) and abortion.

From the outer security perimeter, I made the now familiar half-mile trek to the Pepsi Center, standing in line for over 30 minutes at the magnometers with the other delegates. I stopped in at the media tents (there are five stretched over a square mile) to say hello to the boys, went to the filing center to check my email, and otherwise dawdled my way through a lot of boring speakers until, about 20 minutes before Clinton was set to speak, I decided to head down to the floor.

Bad news, booby. The anticipation over what Clinton would say brought out not only her supporters but waves of curious convention-goers, and the fire marshals closed the floor. Getting past student volunteers on power trips is about as hard as skipping the line at a ski lift. But fire marshals are a different story. I tried all my usual slip holes, but there was a fire marshal at every entry point. I climbed up to the mezzanine level thinking I could enter there and walk down. No dice.

With only eight minutes left, I watched irate delegates from Ohio and Illinois scream at the fire marshal that they were DELEGATES, FOR GOD'S SAKE. "I have a seat in there waiting for me," one woman shouted. But the marshals weren't giving an inch.

These are the times when it pays to be a professional. I glanced around and noticed a well-coifed man in a suit holding the same Floor Pass I had. He was standing in front of an elevator marked NBC. "What floor?" I asked him when we stepped in. "Club level," he said. I punched the button and we exited together.

Just moments before, Bill Clinton stepped out on the same floor and a mob of TV cameras surrounded him. He was going to watch the speech from the CNN suite, but it didn't look like there'd be an extra chair for me. I started walking the circle around to the other media suites: NBC, CBS, BBC, ETC. Each had its own guard and fire marshal. But somewhere down the row, there was a long thin black curtain with no guards and a lot of crowd noise behind it.

I slipped around the stanchion holding the curtain to the wall and found myself in what, during a regular season basketball game, is called the "On The Rocks Spirit Bar."

"What can I get you," the bartender asked.

"A gin and tonic will be fine," I said.

I grabbed my cocktail and stepped through one of the two entryways into the club seat section. No guards. No fire marshal. Who in their right mind is going to close a bar during a convention? All the seats were taken, but there was room in the aisle, just enough room to sit on the step and slide my drink under my legs.

The Locomotive

I don't know who makes these convention videos, but the guy who did Hillary's must have been pretty jacked on Red Bull and No Doze. The opening image was the face of an old steam locomotive (think Thomas The Train) that chugged along like a lot of the other videos pulling up black & white images of her ancestors living the hardscrabble life in order to give birth to her.

Then suddenly, the music shifted and there was Hillary the presidential candidate speaking before this group and that, giving all her famous lines, bits and bites, here and there, living her mother's dream that she could grow up to be anything she wanted to be, shattering the glass ceiling, listening to steelworkers, encouraging children, smiling, waving, brimming with hope . . . and pulling the whole damned women's movement along behind her.

"This is what should have been," a woman standing next to me whispered to her friend.

"Imagine my daughter seeing this," her friend whispered back.

When the video ended and Chelsea introduced her mother, the crowd gave Clinton an exuberant, full-throated five-minute ovation. She walked the stage basking in the adulation, waving and smiling, truly smiling like she meant it.

Hillary Delivers

All that Clinton really had to say she said in the first 30 seconds. "I'm proud to be here tonight. A proud mother. A proud Democrat. A proud American. And a proud supporter of Barack Obama."

As convention whips passed out signs to delegates saying on one side "Unity" and the other either "Obama" or "Hillary,' she gave the Obama people exactly what they wanted. "Whether you voted for me, or voted for Barack, the time is now to unite as a single party with a single purpose," she said. "We are on the same team, and none of us can sit on the sidelines."

And the Obama people gave Clinton a gift in return, the gift of oratory, represented on stage by a little piece of technology Obama has successfully employed throughout the campaign. It consists of two twin see-through teleprompters mounted inches outside the TV shot. With her script now available wherever she turned, Clinton spoke with a confident ease I hadn't seen before, and her words jumped off the page.

"Tonight, we need to remember what a presidential election is really about," she said. "When the polls have closed, and the ads are finally off the air, it comes down to you — the American people, your lives, and your children's futures."

Clinton used this occasion, her swan song of the campaign, to recall all that she learned along the campaign trail, and a good number of the people she met. She brought it all back home when she asked her supporters to ask themselves:

"Were you in this campaign just for me? Or were you in it for that young Marine and others like him? Were you in it for that mom struggling with cancer while raising her kids? Were you in it for that boy and his mom surviving on the minimum wage? Were you in it for all the people in this country who feel invisible?"

And that is the question that lingers. On the eve of the convention, a poll reported that 21 percent of Clinton's supporters in the primaries say they will vote for John McCain, and 27 percent more say they are undecided. If that's true, it's enough to sink any effort Obama can mount this fall.

Hillary has done her part. Now, will her supporters do theirs?

Surprise!

August 28, 2008

In hindsight, I should have seen it coming. The day had gone too smoothly. There was no excitement in the evening convention schedule (unless you consider a speech by Joe Biden exciting) and a convention without excitement is like Christmas without Santa Claus. All business.

Barack Obama formally won the Democratic nomination in an early afternoon roll call that took all of 42 minutes. For all the *sturm und drang* over whether Hillary's delegates would be able to vote their conscience, the vote tallies rolled in as if all the primaries that came before were just a few meaningless intra-squad games: Alabama (Obama 48, Clinton 5), Alaska (Obama 15, Clinton 3), American Samoa (Obama 8.5, Clinton 2.5) and so on until they reached New Jersey (Obama 127, Clinton 0), which put Obama one state shy of going over the top.

New Mexico ("Land of Enchantment") yielded to Illinois ("Land of Lincoln") which yielded in turn to New York ("Land of Many Politicians") where Hillary herself moved that the convention accept Obama's nomination by acclamation.

The band broke out in a joyous version of "Love Train" by the O'Jays:

August 27

Obama nominated in 42 minute roll call with Clinton calling for approval by acclamation

People of the world,
Join hands,
Start a love train,
Love Train . . .

Delegates held hands and swayed side to side. They sang along and seemed relieved that it was over. And that's the way it happened. I swear. You can check the tape.

Bill Clinton's Turn

There was, of course, still one more Clinton to get off the stage before Obama could take his rightful place in the limelight. Former President Bill Clinton led an evening of prime time speeches that would be capped off by the introduction of Obama's vice-presidential running mate Sen. Joe Biden.

The table was set for him by the passing out of thousands of American flags. When he was introduced, Democrats greeted him with a warm wave of applause that went on for several minutes.

"Y'all sit down," he told them. "We gotta get on with the show here." But they kept cheering and waving their flags. "I love this," he said, "but we have important work to do here tonight."

The work for Clinton was to give Obama his blessing, not easy for a man who believes the Obama camp unfairly cast him as a racist, and at the same time remind Democrats that he hadn't been a bad president himself (with one notable exception).

Three times, he reiterated his belief that Obama was "ready" — especially now that he has the "experience and wisdom" of Biden at his side — to carry out an agenda that (if you replaced Obama's name with his own in all the sentences starting "Obama will . . .") looked pretty much like Clinton's.

Oh well, he did what he had to do. This is an expression I learned by watching the cable guys analyze every speech. "But did he do what he had to do?" Wolf Blitzer asks, then the kibitzers on the set chew over each other's opinions until all agree he did what he had to do, and the next speaker hits the stage. All Clinton really had to do was show up and not say anything stupid. So yes, he did what he had to do.

Folks, Meet Joe Biden

Next it was Biden's turn. Despite his 35 years in the Senate, Biden is not a well-known commodity in American politics. If you ask the average voter under the age of 30 what they know about Biden, most will probably recall a *Daily Show* episode last year when Jon Stewart put a ticking clock under a Biden debate answer that ran eight minutes long.

The good thing about not being well-known, from a political handler's perspective, is that you start with a blank slate (and the image you create only has to last for another 66 days until the election is over.) This explains the well-crafted video that brought Biden on stage, the loving introduction by his better-spoken son, and the frequent cutaway shots to his 90-year-old mother, Catherine Biden, who may be the sweetest grandmother in politics since Barbara Bush.

Biden did all right with his prepared remarks. He only wandered off-script a couple times (a trait, by the way, that already has the Obama press office issuing not only prepared remarks but a follow-up "verbatim" version) and he demonstrated that, despite his three decades of friendship with John McCain, he's not afraid to take on the traditional running mate role of attack dog.

As I was sitting in the pressroom scratching my head over what to make of this underplayed historic day, Biden's wife walked onstage to announce she had a special surprise for her husband. Imagine, if you will, the sound of the palm of my hand thunking against my forehead. Why didn't I see it coming?

What's the point of political experience if you can't remember the long tradition of the nominee making a "surprise" appearance at the convention on the night before his Thursday acceptance speech?

Surprise

Viewers at home were given an early warning that Obama was about to appear with "breaking news" screen crawlers in the middle of Biden's speech, what's often called in television "The Tease." But the surprise was a well-kept secret inside the hall. The only hints were a roaming camera on-stage and what seemed to me at the time to be more cameras placed around the hall throwing crowd shots, famous faces and panoramic views of the hall up on the big screen behind the podium.

The stagecraft Obama's media team has brought to the campaign this year has always impressed me. "See how they're moving the shots around," I remarked earlier to a reporter sitting next to me, "It really opens up the hall and humanizes things. These Obama guys are good." Little did I know how good.

When Obama walked out onto the stage to join Biden, prime time coverage was coming to a close. Suddenly, the electricity in the hall jumped 100 volts. "Now you see why I'm so proud to have Joe Biden, Jill Biden, Beau Biden and Mama Biden with me on this journey," Mr. Cool said as the Biden family (all white, might I awkwardly note) surrounded him. He thanked the convention for their great work so far. Wasn't Michelle's speech fantastic? And Hillary, a real trooper, isn't she? And Mr. President, high fives to you. Now let's open this baby up to the rest of America

tomorrow night in Mile High Stadium. Meet me at the 50-yard-line. You ain't seen nothing yet.

To the swell of Bruce Springsteen's "The Rising", Obama walked among his new extended family shaking hands. Cameras picked out the happy faces of Bill, Hillary and Chelsea in the hall; and the networks were left with too little time for commentary, but just enough to linger on the scene until the image was seared into our memory.

Masterful.

Sermon on The 50-Yard Line

August 29, 2008

And the river opens for the righteous.
–Jackson Browne/Steve Van Zandt

THEY CAME BY bus, by light rail, by limousine, and by foot, the true believers. They were not exactly your tired, your poor, your hungry, huddled masses yearning to be free. But after three hours of waiting at the security gates, they were tired and hungry.

They were there for an event that many thought had all the earmarks of a disaster, Barack Obama's acceptance speech before 84,000 people on the last night of the Democratic convention in Mile High Stadium.

Politico's Charles Mahtesian wrote on the eve of the speech that the elaborate stagecraft, teeming crowds and unpredictable weather "have heightened worries that the Obama campaign is engaging in a high-risk endeavor in an uncontrollable environment."

August 28

Obama accepts nomination in speech at Mile High Stadium

August 29

McCain chooses Alaska Gov. Sarah Palin As VP running mate

"A common concern," he wrote, is that the stadium appearance "gives Republicans a chance to drive home their message that the Democratic nominee is a narcissistic celebrity candidate."

Throughout the afternoon, the crowds did, in fact, teem. They stood in security lines for three hours under a blazing sun to get into the stadium. Once they were in, many had to wait five more hours before Obama spoke. All in all, they remained good-natured, entertained by the likes of Will.i.am, Sheryl Crow and Stevie Wonder. If they got up to get a hot dog, they cajoled a neighbor to hold their seat. Even then, the line at the concession stand was another 20–30 minutes.

Although the convention convened at 4:30 in the afternoon, the prime time version — the one that would be broadcast across the country — did not start until 7. And it started slowly with a mixed bag of generals, politicians, ordinary citizens, Democrats and Republicans — everyone from Dwight Eisenhower's granddaughter Susan to a man who reminded people he's not Smith Barney but Barney Smith.

Come the Savior

That brought us up to The Moment — a single hour into which the Democrats poured almost half of the $16 million the federal government gave them to stage this convention — the moment Barack Obama would accept his party's nomination.

It started with a 7-minute film produced by Stephen Spielberg telling the story of Obama's life in words and pictures culled from family albums. The images were warm and fuzzy, the music on the mark. If this Hollywood thing doesn't work out, Spielberg has a great career ahead as a wedding videographer.

Then, without further ado, Obama walked on stage. The stadium erupted.

There is no describing the speech Obama gave on this evening. Political science students will read it in years to come as one of the finest pieces of political oratory in decades. People who were there when he delivered it will remember it for the rest of their lives.

But because we are in the middle of a heated political contest — with the Republicans about to take center stage at a convention of their own next week — I'd like to talk about what Obama did with this speech as much as what he said — because how he did it may well determine whether he wins or loses this presidential campaign.

Read and Discuss

As everyone by now recognizes, Obama is one of those rare politicians who can not only formulate and write down his ideas but think about what he is saying as he says it.

The pauses in his cadence — the absence of superfluous connecting phrases — allow him to deliver, as he did Thursday night, something as simple as an acknowledgement of previous speakers Hillary and Bill Clinton, Ted Kennedy and Joe Biden as if it were The Lord's Prayer.

He set out to tell "my story" using the well-known facts of his Kenyan father and Kansas mother as stepping stones. He characterized his achievement on this night as the fulfillment of their dreams: "that promise that has always set this country apart — that through hard work and sacrifice, each of us can pursue our individual dreams but still come together as one American family, to ensure that the next generation can pursue their dreams as well."

In short, succinct phrases, Obama then encapsulated some of the problems that threaten "the promise" today, laying the blame on "broken politics" in Washington and the failed policies of George W. Bush.

Gradually substituting "we" for "I," he spoke for nearly eight minutes before issuing his first call to action: "America, we are better than these last eight years. We are a better country than this."

With Bush's name now in the mix (and, for good measure, his vice president Dick Cheney's), Obama turned next to the Republicans meeting next week in Minnesota and their nominee, John McCain. Many Democrats, notably Hillary Clinton, have expressed doubts that Obama has the stomach for a rough and tumble political fight with McCain this fall. Now he showed them he could attack, without the rough and tumble.

From this moral high ground of restoring the American promise that Bush destroyed, he noted that McCain voted with the president 90 percent of the time. "On issue after issue that would make a difference in your lives . . . Senator McCain has been anything but independent," he said, striking at one of McCain's strongest claims.

He made his point with questions, not charges, and a backhanded compliment: "Now, I don't believe that Senator McCain doesn't care what's going on in the lives of Americans. I just think he doesn't know. Why else would he define middle-class as someone making under five million dollars a year? . . . How else could he offer a health care plan that would actually tax people's benefits, or an education plan that would do nothing to help families pay for college, or a plan that would privatize Social Security and gamble your retirement?

"It's not because John McCain doesn't care. It's because John McCain doesn't get it."

The Obama Platform

The specifics of what Obama would do if he were president came in the middle of his speech, and took up nearly half of its 50-minute length. But Obama didn't just tick off his talking points. He started by defining "a very different measure of what constitutes progress in this country" that gave him a platform to not only propose programs, but explain why they were important in people's lives.

He rooted his vision for America in the past accomplishments of the Clinton administration, the progressive Democratic tradition of Franklin Roosevelt and, once again, "the promise" that put "my grandfather" through college on the GI bill; the food stamps that fed "my mom" while she sent her kids to the best schools in the land on student loans and scholarships; and "my grandmother," who worked her way up from the secretarial pool to middle-management, despite years of being passed over for promotions because she was a woman.

What an odd but appropriate time to bring up the name of his opponent again, and refute another of McCain's charges against him.

"I don't know what kind of lives John McCain thinks that celebrities lead, but this has been mine. These are my heroes. Theirs are the stories that shaped me. And it is on their behalf that I intend to win this election and keep our promise alive as President of the United States."

Hot Button Issues

Woven throughout Obama's speech was the concept of individual responsibility and mutual responsibility as "the essence of the American promise." One is a tent pole of the Republican party. The other holds up the Democrats. They are represented on the political extremes by Libertarianism and Socialism, and one of Obama's goals in this speech was to advocate these are twin tenets that can — and probably must — co-exist in America.

That will require Democrats and Republicans to "cast off the worn ideas and politics of the past," he said, especially the wedge issues that split the electorate in the 2000 and 2004 campaigns.

* "We may not agree on abortion, but surely we can agree on reducing the number of unwanted pregnancies in this country," he said.

* "The reality of gun ownership may be different for hunters in rural Ohio than for those plagued by gang violence in Cleveland, but don't tell me we can't uphold the Second Amendment while keeping AK-47's out of the hands of criminals," he added.

* "Passions fly on immigration, but I don't know anyone who benefits when a mother is separated from her infant or an employer undercuts American wages by hiring illegal workers," he concluded.

"This too is part of the American promise — the promise of a democracy where we can find the strength and grace to bridge divides and unite in common effort."

Bridging that divide, he said in another part of the speech, will require a new civility in politics.

"So let us agree that patriotism has no party," Obama said. "I love this country, and so do you, and so does John McCain."

If he had left it at that, he might have held that high ground. But I suspect someone, in the cause of toughness, insisted he fortify his position against negative attacks in the fall by adding "So I've got news for you, John McCain. We all put our country first."

Fighting words that will only bring on a fight.

Shades of Martin Luther King

At the end of his speech, Obama segued into the recognition that his speech came on the 45th anniversary of Martin Luther King's "I Have a Dream" speech. He did it so seamlessly no one saw it coming. He never mentioned King by name. Nor did he cite any of the famous lines school children now know by heart.

He started with words he'd spoken before on the primary campaign trail.

"At defining moments like this one, the change we need doesn't come from Washington. Change comes to Washington. Change happens because the

American people demand it — because they rise up and insist on new ideas and new leadership, a new politics for a new time."

Now listen to what he says next — and keep in mind King's "I've Been to The Mountain Top" speech in Memphis:

"I believe that as hard as it will be, the change we need is coming. Because I've seen it. Because I've lived it. I've seen it in Illinois, when we provided health care to more children and moved more families from welfare to work. I've seen it in Washington, when we worked across party lines to open up government and hold lobbyists more accountable . . ."

"This country of ours has more wealth than any nation, but that's not what makes us rich. We have the most powerful military on earth, but that's not what makes us strong. Our universities and our culture are the envy of the world, but that's not what keeps the world coming to our shores."

"Instead, it is that American spirit — that American promise — that pushes us forward even when the path is uncertain; that binds us together in spite of our differences; that makes us fix our eye not on what is seen, but what is unseen, that better place around the bend."

"And it is that promise that 45 years ago today, brought Americans from every corner of this land to stand together on a Mall in Washington, before Lincoln's Memorial, and hear a young preacher from Georgia speak of his dream."

"The men and women who gathered there could've heard many things," Obama continued, the time and place now shifted back to 1963.

"They could've heard words of anger and discord. They could've been told to succumb to the fear and frustration of so many dreams deferred. But what the people heard instead — people of every creed and color, from every walk of life — is that in America, our destiny is inextricably linked. That together, our dreams can be one."

Only then did Obama pull from King's speech a quote. "We cannot walk alone," the preacher cried. "And as we walk, we must make the pledge that we shall always march ahead. We cannot turn back."

There's a little bit of preacher in every president. It comes with the office Teddy Roosevelt once called the bully pulpit. We expect our presidents to embody not only our politics but, in some ways, our moral values. They respond in kind by concluding their remarks "God Bless You, and God Bless the United States."

On this day in Denver, Barack Obama channeled the inner preacher in him out to a television audience estimated at 38 million people. And to prove his clergy cred, he reached into the Bible for a passage in Hebrews 10:23 that is the very definition of hope.

"Let us keep that promise, the American promise" Obama concluded, "and in the words of the Scripture hold firmly, without wavering, to the hope that we confess."

Coda

Now the seats are all empty
Let the roadies take the stage . . .
But when the last guitar's been packed away
You know I still want to play . . .

We've got to drive all night and do a show
In Chicago, or Detroit, I don't know . . .
We just pass the time in our hotel rooms
And wander 'round backstage
Til those lights come up and we hear that crowd
And we remember why we came.

–Jackson Browne

I hope you enjoyed the show. See you in St. Paul.

The Republican Convention: I'm a Blogger

August 31, 2008

THIS WEEK I'M **a blogger.** And not just any blogger. I'm an official Republican Blogger, one of 122 accredited to occupy the lowest rung on the media ladder and the highest seats in the hall.

I picked up my credentials yesterday at the Minneapolis Convention Center, which was a hell of a lot easier to get to than anything in Denver. They identify me as "Special Press" and put me in the company of such Internet luminaries as *The Morning Clacker, The Dead Pelican, Hot Air* and *The Grizzly Groundswell.*

Bloggers are to the Republicans what Katrina victims are to the Democrats — heroic voices washed away in the flood of mainstream media and celebrated for their insignificance.

"We have a great appreciation for bloggers and the ever-increasing role new media has in providing real-time

August 31 – September 4

Republican Convention in St. Paul

September 1

Hurricane Gustav hits New Orleans

Day one speeches at Republican Convention cancelled

information and shaping public opinion," the party says on its website. But when a fellow blogger asked whether her photographer might get a floor pass to be within shooting range, Hayden Pruitt, the new media coordinator said "I wish I could help. This is all I have."

Along with my credentials I got a bag of "Special Press" swag, the contents of which were as follows: A GOP water bottle, UPS breath mints, a gift card from AT&T good for one free ringtone, two Nature Valley health bars, an umbrella, and my favorite: a commemorative box of Kraft Macaroni & Cheese with an elephant on the front holding up a "Republicans in 2008" placard.

Just when I thought it couldn't get better, I found myself swept up in the flow of delegates headed to the opening welcome party. The feature attraction was a traveling exhibit of White House memorabilia. There were dioramas of the Oval office under various presidents, a living replica of the White House rose garden, a collection of White House china and tours of the C-SPAN bus and a replica of Air Force One.

Thousands of delegates lined up to get their picture taken sitting behind

President Bush's desk, standing on the Capitol steps taking the oath of office, or in the company of a live bald eagle. The food was pretty good too.

Day One Cancelled

The fly in the ointment here in Minnesota is Hurricane Gustav, now a category-3 storm hurtling toward New Orleans. While I was driving up from Chicago, John McCain announced that all but the most perfunctory call to order and adopting of rules have been cancelled for the opening session Monday.

President Bush and Vice President Cheney will not be giving speeches (a blessing in disguise given Bush's current 28 percent approval rating). Bush will be overseeing the hurricane relief efforts. Cheney will be in an undisclosed location doing the usual undisclosed things that he does.

What this means for the rest of the week is anyone's guess. "At times like these, we take off our Republican hats and put on our American hats," McCain said when he announced the cancellation. But I haven't seen any significant shift in the hatwear so far.

Many of the larger media organizations have pulled resources out of Minneapolis to cover the Gulf storm. As long as the Republicans keep postponing, the rest of us will have to find stories outside the convention perimeter. There's an anti-war demonstration Monday at the Capitol in St. Paul that is expected to draw 50,000 protesters. And there are, of course, the parties. I'm not worried about lack of subject material. But the Republicans should be. Idle hands are the devil's playground.

The Super 8

I'm stay at the Super 8 motel just outside Minneapolis, which appears to be Ron Paul's convention headquarters. It is tucked away in a little nest of cheap motels behind the Earle Brown Bowling Lanes. The lobby smells like an airport smoking lounge and the room keycard announces that room service is available by calling Domino's.

A dozen copies of *Republic Magazine*, a glossy magazine out of Florida devoted to all things Ron Paul, are scattered around the coffee table at the check-in counter. The clerk says a lot of his supporters are staying here because the first event Monday, A Liberty Leadership Summit, is just across the highway in the Earle Brown Heritage Center. Brown was the farmer who donated the land for the township.

I haul my luggage and swag bag up to the room, tap out a few notes on the computer and crawl into bed. I guess we all know where tomorrow starts.

Going Nowhere, Doing Nuthin'

Sept 2, 2008

I'M BEGINNING TO get the hang of this blogger thing. You wake up. You walk around. Nothing happens. And you write about it.

As promised, I stopped by the Ron Paul Leadership Summit this morning — only to learn that it was a private session closed to the press. "It's like our strategy session. We don't want to be giving it away," one delegate told me. Jeff Greenspan, the southwest regional director for Paul's primary campaign, was more forthcoming.

"The Ron Paul campaign is over. There's nothing planned for November," he said. "But the Campaign for Liberty (a tax-exempt advocacy group that grew out of Paul's race) is our attempt to find people who think like us, and educate and activate them. So we're having this invitation-only day to organize the effort."

Fine by me. Get organized. Get cracking. You Paulettes have a long way to go before you catch up with the Obama machine.

The Anti-War March

Next stop in my busy day was the anti-war march on the grounds of the state capitol in St. Paul. It's been a while since I've been to an anti-war rally — 35 years to be exact — so it was good to see that rally wear hasn't changed.

I was surprised to find a contingent from the Students for a Democratic Society, known in my day as SDS. "Where have you guys been the last 40 years?" I asked one of the students holding up the banner. He gave me one of those 'who's asking?' looks reserved for police spies, but finally decided I was okay.

"We're the new SDS," he said. "We started up again back in 2006 and we're the fastest growing student organizaton in the country. We have chapters on 100 campuses." He reached in his pocket and gave me a "Funk the War" flyer with their website address. "Check it out," he said.

We marched from the state capitol building down to the Xcel Energy Center where the Republicans were meeting. I hung for a while with my new friends from SDS who seemed flummoxed that the guerilla street tactics that worked so well in Chicago in '68 weren't as effective in Minneapolis. "Off the sidewalks and into the streets," one young organizer shouted through his bullhorn. "Come on! Please."

When we passed one of the security checkpoints, I peeled off into the hall. Later I heard that 56 protesters were arrested, probably my guys, most for smashing windows and overturning newspaper boxes.

The View From Section 222

Hurricane Gustav was due to hit New Orleans about the same time the gavel came down on the convention's first day, so I made my way to the blogger gallery in Section 222 to watch the maelstrom.

I was there for Mike Duncan's call to order, the presentation of the colors by the Boy Scouts of the North Star of Minnesota, the pledge of allegiance led by Serena Krishna of Arizona and the singing of the National Anthem by Miss Minnesota 2008, Angela McDermott. (These are the kind of details you can focus on when you are "Special Press" — because you are so near the acoustic speakers in the rafters and so far away from the floor you can't really see anything else.)

Up in Section 222, there was plenty of time to cogitate on the Republicans' predicament, of which Gustav was only the latest reminder.

Gustav was no Katrina, but the Bush administration response to Katrina had been such a disaster John McCain had to make his convention plans as if it could be. On the day Bush was scheduled to endorse him, McCain had to demonstrate how differently he would respond to the same threat.

As the party nominee and not the president, however, there really wasn't much he could do. He packed toilet paper and teddy bears into care packages in Ohio intended for victim relief. He scaled back convention activities Monday to the bare bones so Republicans would not appear to be fiddling while New Orleans burned. He tried, not very effectively, to turn the convention stage into a Red Cross telethon. Every speaker opened with his concern for the people in harm's way, and stage monitors carried the text message address for GIVE 2HELP so people watching on TV (was anyone really watching this on TV?) could make relief contributions.

At the same convention where McCain had to break from the president to show his independence, he had to play alongside him on the same team. He had to hug him, kick him, embrace him and toss him overboard — all in the three days before his acceptance speech — if he wanted to have any chance of winning in the fall.

If there was a high point to Monday's proceedings, it was the joint appearance of Laura Bush and McCain's wife Cindy, an uneasy and hastily arranged way of saying we're all in this together.

The Democrats introduced Michelle Obama on the first day of their convention with a carefully orchestrated crescendo of praise from friends and family. Cindy McCain simply walked on stage wearing a yellow dress that looked like a Ralph Lauren raincoat, repeated her husband's line about wearing American hats instead of Republican hats, and walked off. America, meet your next First Lady. Huh?

The Hurricane Within

With only three days left, it will be interesting to see how fast the Republicans can forget Gustav the intruder. There's talk that somewhere over at the Minneapolis Convention Center delegates are going to be spending their free time packing toiletries into 80,000 "comfort packages" for Gustav victims. But the new story swirling around the hall is Sarah Palin, the little-known Governor of Alaska who McCain has tapped to be his vice-president.

Since McCain announced his choice (only four days ago), reporters have turned her hometown of Wasilla (pop. 9,800) into a happy hunting ground for friends and enemies. The first stories to break talked about her sister's messy divorce and a legislative investigation into her attempts to get her ex-brother-in-law fired as a state trooper. Today, to quell rumors on the Internet, Palin announced her 17-year-old daughter Bristol is five months pregnant, and intends to marry the father.

Palin has yet to show up in Minneapolis to meet the delegates, or the press, but she's scheduled to give her vice-presidential acceptance speech in 36 hours. There's blood in the water, as we used to say back in the pressroom. I think it's time to come down out of Section 222 and take a swim.

The Fisherwoman

September 3, 2008

IT MAY COME as a surprise to some of you, but I am a licensed fisherman. I am authorized in Wisconsin to buy beer, sit in a boat and drown worms in any lake in the state.

Unlike Sarah Palin, I have not taken out the permit needed to do this in the winter through a hole in the ice, but I am familiar with the sight of fishing shacks out on the frozen ice. From now on, whenever I see them, I will think to myself: there are a dozen vice presidents in the making.

Alaska Gov. Palin is the woman of the hour at this Republican convention, the co-pilot John McCain has chosen to play Goose to his Maverick in what is shaping up to be a Republican replay of *Top Gun* in the fall elections.

She has all the necessary qualifications, a quick wit and sharp tongue, down home values cultivated at five colleges before she graduated from Northern Idaho State, and a fearsome desire to take on the entrenched interests in government, whether that's Alaska's Republican establishment or the local librarian trying to stock her shelves with books that Palin feels have inappropriate language.

She also has never played on a stage quite like this. She has been governor of Alaska for only 21 months. Aside from crossing Canada to get to the lower 48, she has only been out of the country once in 2007 to visit Alaskan National Guard troops in Kuwait and Germany. Republicans tout her executive ability, but most of it came during her six years as mayor of Wasilla, whose annual budget at the time of $5.9 million wouldn't cover the catering costs at this convention.

Ever since John McCain surprised the country with his running mate selection, the details of Palin's life have been dribbling out in bits and pieces, not all flattering. What we know now that we didn't know when McCain announced his choice is that the anti-abortion abstinence advocate has a 17-year-old daughter Bristol who is five months pregnant and will be marrying her 18-year-old boyfriend. But that's about all we know. The Alaska governor has still not spoken to the press.

Last fall, well before she was considered vice-presidential material, *Newsweek* sent a reporter to Alaska who came back with this flattering portrait of her on-the-go lifestyle in Alaska. "She calls herself a 'hockey mom' and manages to juggle the lives of her five children (the last, born with Down syndrome, is less than 5 months old) while running the state of Alaska and routinely antagonizing the powers that be."

"The throw rug on her couch is the skin of a grizzly bear shot by her father, a retired teacher turned 'nuisance-control specialist' (varmint hunter for hire) whose pickup truck bears the sticker VEGETARIAN — OLD INDIAN WORD FOR 'BAD HUNTER."

"As she spoke to the reporter, she juggled two BlackBerrys and a cell phone, with one always buzzing. She seemed unfazed, indeed to be having fun. As strands of hair fell from her librarian's bun she deftly executed an intricate 'don't drop the BlackBerry while fixing the bobby pin' maneuver, several times."

"One of Palin's first acts as governor was to sell the governor's jet on eBay. She thought it was wasteful and, besides, couldn't even land on many of the state's short, gravel airstrips . . . She keeps a float plane, along with some snowmobiles, in her backyard in Wasilla. At the governor's mansion in Juneau, she got rid of the chef . . . 'I don't want (my kids) thinking when I'm done being governor that it's normal to have a chef. It's okay for them to have macaroni and cheese."

In announcing Palin's selection, McCain praised her courage in fighting corruption in Alaska. He singled out her refusal to accept a federal earmark of $223 million for the famous Bridge to Nowhere. What he didn't say (nor did he have to) was that her conservative views on abortion, guns and creationism made her a hero to the party's right wing; nor did he mention that his first two choices for the post, Sen. Joe Lieberman and former Pennsylvania Gov. Tom Ridge, were nixed by the likes of Rush Limbaugh because they were not.

For every flattering portrait, however, there is a counter-balancing negative review. *Time* magazine this week sent its reporter back to Wasilla to look into how the former beauty queen (Miss Wasilla 1984) got onto the town council in 1992 and governed as mayor from 1996 to 2002.

Wasilla, it should be noted, is not a town in the proper sense but a series of strip malls along the Mat Su Valley highway 45 miles north of Anchorage with houses scattered behind them along the route. Palin was one of three community leaders in the early 90's who decided that the growing area needed a police department. They supported her election to the town council but after four years she decided that to get the changes she wanted, she had to become mayor, which entailed running against her former best friend and workout partner.

Vicki Naegele, managing editor of the Mat Su Valley *Frontiersman*, said Palin won by injecting abortion and gun ownership rights into the small town politics of the town. "She flew in there like a big city gal, which she is not. It was a strange time and we came out harshly against her."

Once in office, Palin attempted to fire the six department heads who opposed her election (and succeeded in two cases.) She put a gag order on town employees talking to the *Frontiersman*, Naegele said, and made inquiries at the public library about how to go about banning books with inappropriate language.

The *Washington Post* and *New York Times* have also been combing the records for how Palin governed in Alaska. McCain's version of her opposition to the earmarked funds for the bridge is less forthright than he makes out. When Alaska's Republican Sen. Ted Stevens, now under indictment, earmarked the money for it, Palin was an enthusiastic supporter. It was only after she came into the governor's office -- and the costs escalated from $223 to $435 million — that she opposed it. Although she ultimately cancelled the project, Alaska did not give back the money; it diverted it to other highway projects.

In the *Washington Post* yesterday, Paul Kane also reported that, far from being an ardent opponent of earmarks, Palin won $27 million worth of special grants for Wasilla while she was mayor. No federal money flowed into the town when she first came to office in 1996; but after hiring a clout-heavy law firm, Palin started making annual pilgrimages to Washington to win $500,000 for a youth shelter, $1.9 million for a transportation hub, $900,000 for sewer repairs and $15 million for a rail project connecting Wasilla to Girdwood, where Stevens has a home. In 2002, Palin's last year as mayor, Wasilla won $6.1 million in federal earmarks, nearly $1,000 for every citizen in the town.

The *New York Times* has focused its investigation on an on-going state legislative probe into whether Palin, as governor, used her influence to have Alaska Public Safety Commissioner Walter Monegan fired for refusing to dismiss a state trooper, Mike Wooten, who was going through a messy divorce with her sister.

The McCain staff says the matter has been fully vetted. There are emails from Palin prior to her winning the governorship in which she attests that she overheard Wooten threatening her father and sister. She is not directly linked to any contact with Monegan about the matter, but her husband Todd is. The probe, called Troopergate, is being conducted by a bi-partisan committee of the legislature. Its report is due out October 31 — four days before the general election.

As you can imagine, all this swirl of publicity makes tonight's speech by Palin a much anticipated event. Although the governor has been in Minneapolis since Monday, she hasn't visited any of the state delegations. Few of the delegates know her personally or have any knowledge of what she stands for other than what came out in the initial announcement.

But the very fact the *Times* and the *Post* are raising questions about her background has these delegates gleefully coming to her defense. "Some Washington pundits and media big shots are in a frenzy over the selection of a woman who has actually governed rather than just talked a good game on the Sunday talk shows and hit the Washington cocktail circuit," Fred Thompson told the convention Tuesday night.

"Well, give me a tough Alaskan Governor who has taken on the political establishment in the largest state in the Union [editor note: pop. 683,000] over the beltway business-as-usual crowd any day of the week. And I can say without fear of contradiction that she is the only nominee in the history of either party who knows how to properly field dress a moose . . . with the possible exception of Teddy Roosevelt."

To conventioneers starved for action after Hurricane Gustav stunted the first day's proceedings, it was the kind of red meat declaration that brought down the house. And you can bet Palin will get a similar reaction tonight.

But what's going to happen at the press conference tomorrow, if it happens at all?

Loser Night

September 4, 2008

MAYBE WE DON'T pay enough attention to the losers in these presidential races, those intrepid politicians who, but for a slip of the tongue here or an empty wallet there, might be standing on stage at this Republican convention themselves accepting their party's nomination.

The parade of Republican losers started Tuesday night with a speech by former Sen. Fred Thompson that set the hall afire. Had he shown that kind of passion during the primary season, he might have had a different role at this convention. Maybe he's discovered that the first rule of politics is you have to show up, or maybe he needed the inspiration of a candidate he really believes in, his friend John McCain.

Thompson lent his voice of God to retelling the story of John McCain's travails in the U.S. Navy: his brush with death in a fire on the U.S.S. Forrestal, his capture and captivity in a North Vietnamese prison camp, and his refusal to buckle under the harshest of circumstances. People wept. People clung to their flag pins. Then Thompson turned his oratory on the Democrats.

"There has been no time in our nation's history since we first pledged allegiance to the American flag when the character, judgment and leadership of our President was more important," he intoned.

"To deal with these challenges the Democrats present a history-making nominee for president," he said. "History making in that he is the most liberal, most inexperienced nominee to ever run for president. Apparently they believe that he would match up well with the history-making Democrat controlled Congress. History-making because it is the least accomplished and unpopular Congress in our nation's history."

When the convention resumed Wednesday night, Mitt Romney, Mike Huckabee and Rudy Giuliani stood up to take their whacks. Only Guiliani squeaked into the prime time window of broadcast TV, and Mitt Romney, for one, should be glad because he gave one of the silliest speeches at either convention.

Mr. Machine Will Say Anything

In the short span of 24 hours, the assignment for the losers had shifted from attacking Barack Obama to defending vice presidential nominee Sarah Palin from an "elite media" intent on digging out the details of her past.

Romney wasted little time in getting down to it. "You know, for decades now, the Washington sun has been rising in the East. You see, Washington has been looking to the Eastern elites, to the editorial pages of the *Times* and the *Post,* and to the broadcasters from the coast," he said as the applause drowned out the end of the sentence. "If America really wants to change, it's time to look for the sun in the West, because it's about to rise and shine from Arizona and Alaska."

This was an odd message coming from a Boston investment banker and former governor of Massachusetts with a net worth of $240 million. It got even odder as Romney tried to sort out the differences between a liberal and a conservative. He called a Supreme Court dominated by recent Bush appointees "liberal" for granting constitutional rights to Guantanamo prisoners. He charged that government spending, which has risen 80 percent since Bush took office, was a "liberal" inheritance. And he urged voters to "throw out big government liberals and elect John McCain," ignoring the fact McCain would be replacing that paragon of conservatism, George Bush.

Somewhere in the middle of his peroration, Romney lost the crowd to the concession stand. His speech had all the substance of a cellophane bag. David Gergen, trying to put the best face on it in his CNN commentary, called it "a great speech — for the 1970's."

I Like Mike

The Republicans were fortunate that Romney was followed by former Arkansas Gov. Mike Huckabee. He carried forward the attack on the media and brought the crowd back to life with his usual good humor.

"I'd like to begin by doing something a little unusual," Huckabee said. "I'd like to thank the elite media for doing something that, quite frankly, I didn't think could be done — and that's unifying the Republican party and all of America in support of Sen. McCain and Gov. Palin. The reporting of the last few days has proven tackier than a costume change at a Madonna concert."

Before the laughter could die down, Huckabee slipped smoothly into how his upbringing in a poor household that could afford only Lava soap made him a Republican. "I was in college before I learned it wasn't supposed to hurt when you take a shower." He boldly restated his opposition to abortion. "Every human life has value from the moment of conception." And found a way to endorse Palin without going too far out on the limb. "She got more votes running for mayor of Wasilla [editor note: 1,100] than Joe Biden got running for president this year."

If John McCain should falter in this election cycle, Romney and Huckabee are likely opponents in 2012. On this night, there was no question who won — because Huckabee knows how to tell a joke.

Wandering Off

Somewhere during the musical interlude with John Rich and Cowboy Troy, I wandered off the convention floor (I have, by the way, long ago given up on Section 222.) into the maze of media accommodations next to the convention hall. That's where I found the Diageo Captain's Lounge just outside the radio/TV pressroom. Why I didn't think of this sooner is beyond me.

Diageo — makers of Captain Morgan rum, Glenlivet scotch and Guinness beer — is the official host for the media at the conventions. Next to a spread of finger foods (meatballs, guacamole, trail mix), it runs two non-stop bars with free drinks for the press and televisions scattered around the bar so they can watch the proceedings. The place was packed. Producers, engineers, production assistants, engineers, even a few reporters, mixed freely with delegates taking a break from the action.

What better excuse could I have to order up a cold one and watch the rest of these losers? How else would I see that throughout the night Cindy McCain, Todd Palin and his daughter Willow were playing an elaborate game of pass the baby with Palin's son Trig? That Bristol's new fiancé Levi was nervously chewing gum? Or that Bristol bit her lip when she

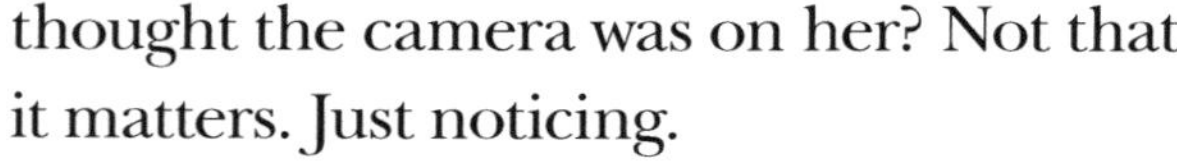

thought the camera was on her? Not that it matters. Just noticing.

The Keynoter

Rudy Giuliani is an acquired taste, and it may be that I've just had my fill. He's not "America's Mayor" anymore — Sarah Palin is. Having spent $34 million running for president, and gaining not a single convention delegate, his vaunted reputation for fiscal responsibility and sound management is in question. And yet, he used his keynote address to frame the presidential race as a job application — like he was Jack Welch interviewing prospects for the next CEO of General Electric.

But Giuliani is no Jack Welch. He was on this night a happy warrior in the Republican cause, amusing himself with snide attacks on his enemy that stretched the bounds of credulity. He took his shots at the press. "We the people get to decide our next president, not the media, not the Hollywood celebrities, not anyone else." Then he took aim at Obama, "a celebrity senator . . . (who has) never run a city, never run a state, and never run a business."

Giuliani sneered at Obama's voting record in the Illinois legislature, repeating an old canard that his votes of "present" — an old Illinois parliamentary maneuver — demonstrated an unwillingness to make decisions. He scoffed at Obama's work as a community organizer among laid off steelworkers in Chicago (followed by a magna cum laude degree from Harvard Law School and 12 years teaching Constitutional law at the University of Chicago.) "What's a community organizer do?" he asked. Then he took a jab at Obama's 300 foreign policy advisors, made the perfunctory charge of flip-flopping, and heralded the McCain-Palin team as the most experienced pair of politicians to ever offer up themselves for public office.

He was at the end of his speech so far off into the deep end of partisanship the delegates stopped rewarding his lines with applause. They just wanted him to stop talking so they could hear Palin, but he wouldn't stop. He prattled on, as if no one in his right mind would vote for those scoundrel Democrats, leaving the mistaken impression this fall election would be a cakewalk — just like his own campaign.

Oh Yeah, Sarah Palin Spoke

I was not as breathless in my appreciation of Sarah Palin's introductory speech to America as the cable commentators, but I did admire her poise in delivering it. Good speechwriters and two days of rehearsal with a teleprompter go a long way toward instilling confidence in any speaker who takes the national stage.

CNN's Wolf Blitzer, who seems to be covering this convention like a home run derby, quickly pronounced, "She hit it out of the park." Chris Matthews on MSNBC called it "a very appealing presentation to Norma Rae America" and "a cultural challenge to Obama." Chris Wallace on Fox bluntly told his Democratic guest Howard Wolfson, "You got problems."

Palin's speech consisted of lines written and lines delivered, some with a stiletto's grace:

"This is a man (Obama) who can give an entire speech about the wars America is fighting, and never use the word 'victory' except when he's talking about his own campaign," she said. "But when the cloud of rhetoric has passed . . . when the stadium lights go out, and those Styrofoam Greek columns are hauled back to some studio lot — what exactly is our opponent's plan? What does he actually seek to accomplish, after he's done turning back the waters and healing the planet?"

I'm still waiting for the press conference, as are most of the media (elite and otherwise.) "What she did was introduce herself to the American people in a very engaging and winning way," NBC anchor Brian Williams cautioned. "But she's someone who is going to be one heartbeat away from the presidency. So we're going to have to see how this plays out in the campaign."

The Balloons Did Not Fall

September 5, 2008

FOR A MAN with so much at stake, John McCain was ill served last night by the party that nominated him, the handlers that staged his acceptance speech, and his own instincts on what to say. Even the balloons did not fall on cue.

Too many in the hall trusted too much that the old man would somehow pull it out. The delegates had their catharsis Wednesday night when his vice presidential nominee Sarah Palin swept them away with a winning smile. She was the Republican Party they wanted to be — young, pretty, brimming with small town conservative values, and yes, like McCain, a defiant maverick. (The idea that the media didn't cotton to her was just an added bonus.)

With her selection, McCain won back the hearts of many Republicans who only 12 months ago wanted to see him dead and buried in the ground. Her choice unified them behind him. They were ready Thursday to show up,

September 4

McCain accepts Republican nomination

September 7

Gallup Daily Tracking Poll

McCain 48 %
Obama 45 %

Fannie Mae and Freddy Mac placed in federal conservatory

applaud McCain for his leadership and get to the party afterwards. But McCain wasn't going to give them victory that easily.

As vividly as other speakers had told the tale of McCain's valor in the prison camps of North Vietnam, he wanted to tell them again in his own words how those travails shaped the man standing before them. "A lot of prisoners had it worse than I did. I'd been mistreated before, but not as badly as others . . . I was tough enough to take it. But after I turned down their offer, they worked me over harder than they ever had before . . . for a long time. And they broke me," he said.

"When they brought me back to my cell, I was hurt and ashamed. Through taps on a wall," he recalled, his cellmate Bob Craner "told me to get back up and fight again for our country and for the men I had the honor to serve with because every day they fought for me."

"I fell in love with my country when I was a prisoner in someone else's," he went on. "I loved it not just for the many comforts of life here. I loved it for its decency, for its faith in the wisdom, justice and goodness of its people. I loved it because it was not just a place but an idea, a cause worth fighting for. I was never the same again. I wasn't my own man anymore. I was my country's."

In his speech, McCain used the word "fight" 33 times.

"In my life, no success has come without a good fight," he said. He's fought against corruption, big spenders, Indian lobbyists, crooked deals, tobacco companies, trial lawyers, drug companies and union bosses. He's fought for better schools, more troops in Iraq, more jobs in America, "and to restore the pride and principles of our party." He's fought "for the fun of it" as a young naval pilot and "for you" in this campaign. "I don't mind a good fight," he said. "But I learned an important lesson along the way. In the end, it matters less that you can fight. What you fight for is the real test."

What also matters in this campaign is whether you inspire enough others to fight alongside you. On that score, McCain spoke to an impatient audience that yearned to make his speech into a pep rally. They shouted "USA" to the parts of his speech they liked and "Boo" to his partisan attacks on his opponent's support of higher taxes, closed markets, increased government spending and bureaucratic health care.

But for the vast majority of the speech, however, they were politely silent while he tried to explain why he wanted to be president.

An Uphill Climb

St. John left St. Paul this week with his party behind the ticket, but the latest polls show only 28 percent of American voters identify themselves as Republicans. How the rest of America perceives the ticket (this week, at least) depends on the impact McCain's delivery had on television. On that score, his stage managers did him no favors.

McCain delivered much of his speech in a close-up shot against a jarring green backdrop. When the camera widened out, it was revealed to be the lawn of the non-descript Walter Reed Junior High School in North Hollywood, California (a snafu engineered by a technician who thought he was grabbing an image of Walter Reed Hospital).

Some people mistakenly thought it was one of McCain's mansions. Republican tactician Karl Rove, after pronouncing the speech "workman like" on Fox TV, ridiculed the choice. "It looked like the Tri Delt sorority house at Stanford."

Indeed, the whole convention floor looked like the Tri Delt house at Stanford. This convention was the whitest in 40 years. Only 36 of the 2,381 delegates were African-American. The music that wafted through the hall all week was a mixture of bop-she-bop and country & western. Delegates in golf shirts and tailored suits took every opportunity to dance to their favorites.

When McCain finished his speech, only a slow trickle of confetti rained down to celebrate. Five of the 50 bags stuffed with 10,000 balloons released, but the rest remained stubbornly lodged in the rafters. (This happened to the Democrats as well in 2004 when CNN caught the stage manager shouting, "Why the hell is nothing falling. What the fuck are you guys doing up there?")

Eventually, about half the balloons came down. By then, the TV commentators had moved on to the post-game analysis of what was deemed by consensus an unremarkable speech.

It's Friday. The party's over. We move to the fall elections with a clear choice between a 72-year-old war hero running on his record and a 47-year-old reformer promising change — and much that is not clear.

But hey, that's why they make you play the game. Talk's cheap, let's race!

Detour Along The Campaign Trail

September 19, 2008

THIS HAS NOT been a good week for politics.

John McCain is stumbling all over himself trying to ride the bump of Sarah Palin. Barack Obama is playing rope-a-dope again. The country is going to hell in a handbasket, and we're arguing about lipstick on a pig.

Last Week, As I Recall

There was more lipstick than pig in last week's exchange of media salvos. The McCain camp accused Obama of teaching sex education to kindergarteners for supporting a bill in the Illinois legislature urging teachers to warn their students against sexual predators. (In my day, we said, "don't get in a car with strangers.") And the Obama camp returned fire with an ad saying McCain was so out of touch he didn't know how to use a computer. (Ignoring the fact that McCain, after having both arms broken in a

Hanoi prison, can't lift his arm above his shoulder without pain, much less text message on a BlackBerry.)

All in all, a lot of sound and fury signifying nothing.

September 10

McCain releases ad criticizing Obama for lipstick on a pig comment

Miss Wasilla

Fortunately, we had Sarah Palin to distract us. She gave her first "exclusive" interview to Charlie Gibson on ABC. Tina Fey, in a spot-on impersonation, mocked it in a Saturday Night Live skit. *People* magazine gave her its cover. And *The National Enquirer* devoted not one, but three stories to her son's drug use, her daughter's wild partying, and her alleged affair with her husband's former business partner (in descending order of plausibility).

September 11

ABC's Charles Gibson does first media interview with Sarah Palin

Clearly, there's a deep reservoir of unknowns about this candidate, and only 48 days left to drill it.

Rick Davis, McCain's campaign manager, said he's not willing to subject Palin to the scrutiny of the mainstream media until they show the proper "respect and deference."

September 12

After McCain ad claims Obama favors sex education for kindergartners, Obama releases ad saying McCain is so out of touch he can't use a computer.

But the floodgates are open. Palin herself opened them when she claimed she was always against The Bridge to Nowhere when she clearly was not. Her vehement support of "no earmarks" is undermined by the fact that, as mayor of Wasilla, she was one of the worst offenders. And now, her knowledge of foreign affairs appears to be limited to what she can see out her front window. It will not take one press conference to unravel her worldview. It will take ten. But she is still avoiding the press.

Alaskans Know Best

The best reporting on Palin so far is coming from people in Alaska who know her. It is less about the specifics of her political philosophy than the context in which it was formed. In a *Newsweek* piece called "Where the Bars Are Open Til 5 a.m.," Amanda Coyne, editor of alaskadispatch.com describes Palin's native Wasilla:

At the Republican convention, Sarah Palin talked about her hometown as if it were a place painted by Norman Rockwell . . . But hardly anything like that exists in Wasilla.

You certainly can have a great time swigging beer in two bars that are allowed to stay open until 5 a.m. It was Mayor Palin who rejected attempts to make them close earlier . . . But once you leave, you might want to watch your back: in a state that is consistently in the top 10 of the nation's most violent per capita.

Wasilla is not a bad place. Families go to church services on Sunday; they gather for picnics, barbecues and town meetings; parents root for their kids at ballgames. It's just not the gauzy, idyllic place of long-neglected "values" that Palin evokes. Rather, it's an unexceptional, gritty town, bisected by a four-lane highway. Along the road, used car lots sit next to car repair shops next to fast-food joints next to pawnshops.

"It's a very confusing place," concedes Wasilla city planner Jim Holycross. "There's no center here. There's no sense of identity.

September 13

Tina Fey does Palin impersonation on *Saturday Night Live*

September 15

Lehman Brothers collapses, Dow falls 504 points

September 16

Insurance giant AIG receives $85 billion federal rescue loan

September 18

Dow drops another 449 points

There's nothing to ground the town. In fact, when I first came here, I got lost looking for the town until I realized I was in the town."

Don't Watch the Polls

Davis continues to believe Palin is a game changer. A surprise, a social conservative, and, as a woman, someone who can stand in as the Republican Hillary Clinton, Palin has brought new life to a tired campaign.

The Gallup daily tracking poll — as good an indicator as any, and that's not saying much — showed Obama rising to an 8-point lead over McCain the day after the Democratic convention; then McCain ending his Republican convention with a 5-point lead. That is, effectively, a 13-point swing in public opinion in less than a week.

Only eight days later, the Gallup results have once again stabilized into a 47-47 dead heat.

Personalities vs. Issues

One of the ways Rick Davis hopes to change the race is to focus voter attention on the personalities of the candidates. "This election is not about issues," he told a gathering of *Washington Post* editors. "This election is about a composite view of what people take away from these candidates, their values, their character, their opinions, their principles."

There's more than a little historical evidence to show Davis is onto something.

President Bush came into office in 2000 because people felt more comfortable with his persona than the stiff Al Gore (that, and a Supreme Court decision). In 2004, Bush won re-election, even as public sentiment was turning against the Iraq War, because of a general discomfort with the Brahmin persona of John Kerry.

Voters like to think there is someone making decisions in the White House who is just like them, although that is rarely the case. Davis is happy to have people vote for their next president based on who is most like me, John McCain or Barack Obama, because 70 percent of those voters are white.

More Distractions

At the height of Palinmania, Davis may have overplayed his hand with quickie TV commercials (run largely on the Internet) challenging Obama on little things — like lipstick on a pig and kindergarten sex education — that added nothing to the national conversation.

On ABC's *The View*, Joy Behar called McCain out for adding "I approve this message" to these lies. "They're not lies," McCain responded feebly. By the end of the week, dozens of newspaper editorial pages had denounced the ads as foul balls. Even Karl Rove, appearing on Fox TV Sunday, had to admit McCain went over the line of "100 percent truthfulness."

September 19

Treasury Sect. Henry Paulson proposes $700 billion bailout package for banks and financial institutions

September 24

McCain suspends campaign to fly to Washington to resolve financial crisis.

September 25

White House summit breaks down; House Republicans scuttle bailout plan the next day

Let Sarah Run, Unfettered and Free

But the McCain camp also now has the difficult task of rolling Palin out on her own, without bringing the media down on her head.

Citing the excitement Palin has brought to the campaign and his large crowds, McCain has kept Palin at his side most of the week.

He gives his speech proclaiming the voters now can get two mavericks for the price of one; and she chimes in with lines cloned off the acceptance speech his speechwriters gave her. If ever there was a dog and pony show, this is it. Half the press says he's riding her coattails and the other half thinks she's hiding under his. No one knows what she really believes because Palin never gets beyond the talking points.

What binds them together is beyond me. Maybe McCain sees Palin as the future of a party he cannot lead. Maybe Palin sees McCain as a father figure who articulates ideas she cannot. In either case, McCain seems to have decided he cannot let Palin speak to the media alone, so we are treated now to the spectacle of joint interviews where they lavish praise on each other, but all the body language says McCain would rather be doing anything else but this.

Back to Reality

There's nothing like a 500-point drop in the stock market to refocus your attention on what matters. What is roiling the markets on Wall Street these days are complex financial transactions beyond the mental capacity of most of us. And, probably, beyond the capacity of John McCain or Barack Obama to fix.

The upheaval is a powerful reminder of all the other things that have gone wrong in the Bush Administration: The tax cuts that brought no economic stimulus. An expensive and pointless war in Iraq. Ballooning federal expenditures, volatile oil prices, a stalled energy package, and the breakdown of fundamental government functions like the hurricane relief effort response to Katrina, to name only a few.

Polls have consistently shown over the last 18 months a record number of Americans believe our country is on the wrong track. Now we have an even deeper discontent: a widespread belief that no one knows how to get us out of this mess.

The need to change the dynamics in Washington — "to change the way Washington does business" — was a powerful enough message in the primaries to catapult Obama to the Democratic nomination, and over the summer McCain too adopted the change mantra.

With only 48 days left to the election, both sides have now put their cards on the table as to how they will do that.

The Case for McCain

McCain goes into the fall as a budget cutter. Bloated and irresponsible government spending has long been a Republican target, but McCain attacks it with more gusto than most. With Palin at his side, these two mavericks are going to knock heads, cut waste, study problems, appoint better people, and find bi-partisan solutions.

The greedy people who caused this fiscal crisis, and the Washington laggards who let it happen will be out of there. And John McCain, he assures crowds, will fight them to his death (no idle threat given how many times, politically and literally, he has eluded it).

The Case for Obama

Barack Obama hopes to live longer than that.

Obama has placed his trust in voters seeing the problem as more than a series of bad decisions by incompetent people. For all the criticism he takes as a cool, cerebral politician who talks in big ideas 35,000 feet above the heads of the people who are suffering, he's defined the central issue as a systemic problem.

His proposed solutions on complex tax questions are far more detailed and well-thought out than McCain's — even those who disagree on principle agree on this — but you have to go their websites to understand the full extent of the differences.

This sometimes hamstrings Obama in the 24/7 news cycle (where Davis is a master of creating hot button issues) but it also gives him more leeway to govern if he is elected.

On the stump, you'll have to settle for Obama's wry sense of humor about the dilemma of the day. In Elko (Nev.) yesterday, Obama chided McCain for saying the solution to the Wall Street crisis was to take on the "The Old Boys Network in Washington."

"This is an 11th hour conversion," he said. "This is somebody who's been in Congress for 26 years, who put seven of the most powerful lobbyists in Washington in charge of his campaign. And now he tells us that he's the one who's going to take on the Old Boys Network. The Old Boys Network? In the McCain campaign, that's called a staff meeting."

Keep in mind as we near the finish line, McCain wants you to decide this race based on who you think will represent your interests in Washington. Obama wants you to cast your vote based on what kind of government you want to be represented in.

And that puts the burden on you to decide not only who you want to lead, but where you want to go, and how to get there.

Don't Let The Door Hit You On The Way Out

September 26, 2008

IT WAS NO fireside chat.

When President Bush stepped out of the shadow of his Treasury Secretary Henry Paulson Wednesday night to address the nation about the meltdown on Wall Street, he read the words off a teleprompter like a beady-eyed robot programmed to remain calm. This time, there was no room to stray off into that sing-song Texas swagger he's used so many times before to lull America into thinking everything is okay.

Everything is not okay. This is one crisis he can't talk his way out of. Not with hope, not with fierce determination, and not with "an abiding faith in the goodness of the American people." This is a catastrophic mess "that came about over many years," he explained without mentioning the last eight of which constituted his presidency.

But what does he care? In four months, he's out of here. And none too soon.

The MBA President

September 26

1st Presidential Debate in Oxford, Mississippi. McCain reverses himself and attends

Sarah Palin gives second interview to CBS Katie Couric

September 29

Bailout package rejected in House

Dow falls 778 points

September 30

Obama breaks 50% barrier in polls; Axelrod calls last two weeks turning point in campaign

It seems funny now to think that Bush came into office as the first president to get a master's degree in business administration — from Harvard, no less. His governing style was to surround himself with a crackerjack management team: Dick Cheney, the steady hand of experience, as his vice-president; Donald Rumsfeld, the no-nonsense contrarian, as Secretary of Defense; Paul O'Neill, the former head of Alcoa Aluminum, Secretary of Treasury; Colin Powell, hero of the Gulf War, Secretary of State.

His predecessor Bill Clinton loved to immerse himself in the minutia of every decision. Bush liked to see ideas flow up through channels. His minions would develop policy then, in the executive office with a few key advisors, he would be "The Decider." At the moment of his first election, what he would decide was still up in the air.

A Republican Washington

Bush ran for office on a promise to lower taxes, cut spending, and reduce federal interference in business. The first round of Bush tax cuts were a no-brainer. A booming economy under Clinton left Bush with a $263 billion budget surplus. Al Gore unsuccessfully argued during the campaign that money should be placed in a Social Security "lock box" to preserve the system for future generations. The Republican controlled House and Senate sided with Bush on lower taxes, but made few attempts to cut spending, thus setting up the false premise we could have our cake and eat it too.

Bush also made good on his promise to reduce government interference, helped along by a package of banking bills developed by Republican Sen. Phil Gramm and signed into law by President Clinton in 1999. They effectively deregulated the financial institutions now in jeopardy, providing the framework for what oversight there is in today's market, but the people and policies that implemented this change were all Bush's.

On the foreign policy front, Bush ran against the Clinton administration's efforts at "nation building" in Bosnia because, he said, too many troops were committed over too long a period to a costly foreign venture that ate up too much money that could be better spent at home.

There were other planks in the Bush platform of 2000, but what carried him into the presidency (aside from a Supreme Court decision on the Florida recount) was the overarching belief that he would "restore integrity" to the oval office.

A Breath of Fresh Air

There was a kind of national relief when Bush took office in January 2001. The long national nightmare of the Monica Lewinsky Affair was over. Whatever residual resentments lingered from the Bush-Gore race, the one thing everyone knew for sure was that this born again Christian wouldn't be getting blowjobs in the oval office any time soon.

What few realized at the time was that Christian values have little to do with politics, especially as they are practiced by the lobbying firms on K Street.

While the media focused on the high profile appointments to Bush's cabinet, the lower ranks in the multitude of federal agencies and commissions were being filled with political appointees chosen by Bush's political strategist Karl Rove for their contributions to the party.

With firm control of the House, Senate and White House, Republicans led by Rep. Tom DeLay made sure the lobbying firms along K Street hired Republicans. Their reward was easy access to dozens of federal agency administrators, control over writing industry regulations (in the name of less government interference) and special interest spending—lots of spending, for a prescription drug bill, earmarks, oil exploration, defense contractors, Indian casinos, agricultural subsidies and programs tucked so deeply into the federal budget many congressmen still don't know they are there.

September 11th

The common saying is that the September 11th attack on the World Trade Center "changed everything." It certainly had far-reaching repercussions in the hunt for Osama bin Laden, the invasion of Afghanistan and Iraq, the creation of a Homeland Security Department, military prisons in Guantanamo, domestic surveillance, foreign intelligence and, as important as all those, how safe Americans feel in an unstable world.

It also set in motion a political offensive designed by the Bush White House to convince Americans some things about his war on terrorism were so important they could not be shared with the people. We'd just have to trust our leaders to do the right thing.

That trust led to a strong Republican victory in the 2002 congressional elections and Bush's own re-election in 2004, and in the betrayal of that trust lie the seeds of skepticism about the Bush administration today.

The Iraq War

History's verdict on the Bush administration will come by and large out of his decision to invade Iraq, and it will be a complicated verdict because all the consequences of that war are still not known. What we do know is that debate over that war has dominated the national conversation for the last five years. It was the deciding issue in the 2004 presidential election and in 2008 the candidates of both parties won their nominations based on their very different views of how that war is going.

We also know that the Iraq War has consumed us as a nation. Hundreds of thousands of soldiers have cycled through Iraq with 4,000 returning in body bags and tens of thousands coming back with crippling injuries. National guard deployments have disrupted families. Our veterans' health facilities are over-extended. Public opinion on the war is fractured. And the cost . . . does anybody know the real cost? Is it the conservative $800 billion to date or the projected $3 trillion by the time we leave?

The biggest casualty of the Iraq War has been the United States government itself. Bush's initial instinct that nation building is both costly and distracting has proven prescient. If only he had listened to himself. Instead, 9/11 and the Iraq War created a climate of secrecy in Washington where no decision is transparent.

The Slow Seepage of Corruption

It may have started as early as Bush's first year when Vice President Cheney convened a task force of oil company executives to "solve" the energy crisis, then refused to disclose their names or proceedings. Maybe it started when disgraced lobbyist Jack Abramoff, later convicted of shaking down Indian casinos for bribe money, slipped in and out of the White House 200 times in 2001 and 2002 looking for favors. Or when the House passed a 14,000-page prescription drug package loaded with drug company favors at 3 in the morning — and its chief proponent Rep. Billy Tauzin (R-La.)left his House seat to become the $2.5 million a year chief lobbyist for the Pharmaceutical Research and Manufacturers trade group.

A secretive White House has rippled out to a secretive Congress and a tangle of interlocking relationships between congressmen, lobbyists, presidential appointees and, yes, both candidates now running for president on the promise they will change Washington.

There's no telling this week whether Secretary Paulson can get the deal done, or who might pop up to put his foot in the spokes, or why. There's no telling at this point what that deal even consists of. Paulson is asking Congress to trust he will make a good faith effort to resolve this financial crisis, but there is no faith.

There is a popular feeling afoot that maybe we should just let the Wall Street lenders go down and hope they take Washington with them. Enough senators and representatives on both sides of the aisle have stood up to endorse a bailout, however, to convince me there's a need to find a real solution (in an area where I'm no expert).

In his 12-minute speech to the nation, President Bush did not. He has lost the capacity to lead. But who cares? He's history.

Watching Alone

October 3, 2008

JEFF GREENFIELD, THE well-traveled political pundit, once told me in the spin room of the last 2004 presidential debate that he hates spin rooms.

Greenfield has his choice of any seat in the house at a presidential debate — the auditorium, the pressroom or the broadcast booth. But he said he'd rather sit in a quiet room and watch alone.

"The way to watch a debate is the same way 40, 50, 60 million other Americans do — on television — so you can see what they see. The day somebody walks in here and says 'my guy blew it' or Karl Rove appears and says 'I'm dead. I better start looking for a new job,' I might change my mind. But I don't expect that any time soon."

Debate Watching Parties

I mention Greenfield because I was invited to attend a debate watching party to see John McCain and Barack

Obama go at it in the first presidential debate at Ole Miss. Debate watching parties are all the rage this year. Both campaigns are using their Internet social networks to set them up. If you are not affiliated with either campaign, don't despair. As an undecided voter, you are an especially prized guest.

Call your the local TV station and they will happily invite you to watch the debate in a room where they will give you an approval meter to record your every twitch and ask you to raise your hand at the end to indicate who you think won.

October 2

Palin-Biden hold vice-presidential debate

Senate resurrects $700 billion bailout — with $150 billion in corporate tax breaks tagged on

October 3

House approves Senate version of bailout

October 4

McCain pulls advertising in Michigan

Palin charges Obama "pals around with terrorists"; crowds shout "kill him."

Who Won?

Judging who "won" a debate is as much a part of these parties as watching the debate. It seems somehow beyond the comprehension of most Americans that political debates are not sports contests.

There are three presidential debates (and one vice-presidential debate) this year before the November election. For the astute political strategist, each is a 90-minute opportunity on prime time television to build a foundation under the candidate that makes people comfortable voting for him when it counts — Election Day.

You do not win an election by winning two out of three debates. I guess you can sort of win by leading in the next day's political polling. But, as we've seen throughout this campaign, the daily polls fluctuate wildly. And which poll are you going by?

Sorry, I'm Thinking

My wife was eager to attend the party. Her book club (which, as an aside, almost never talks about the books) thinks this would be a good way to get all the husbands and wives together and a lot of "political types will be there," she said. "Wouldn't it be fun to hear what they all have to say?"

"No," I said, "I know what they're going to say."

"So should I tell them you can't come because you're writing?"

"I'm not writing."

"Well, what should I tell them?"

"Tell them I'm thinking."

Office Pool Bets

I succumb to the lure of second-guessing the professionals as much as the next guy. Sports fans have their Fantasy Football. We have our Fantasy Politics.

So my drop-in-the-pot guess in the office betting pool before Friday's presidential debate was that Obama would be eight points ahead of McCain in Monday's Gallup daily tracking poll. This was based more on McCain's clumsy intervention in the Washington bailout negotiations than any high expectations for Obama's performance — and it only costs $5.

October 7

63 million watch 2nd presidential debate

Gallup Poll shows only 9% of Americans think country on the right track

If you couldn't wait until Monday, there were other ways to bet on the outcome. Liberals watching the debate could take comfort in an instant CBS poll Friday night that said 40 percent of viewers thought Obama won, 22 percent thought McCain won, and 38 percent called it a tie. Conservatives watching Fox TV rejoiced because, out of the 58,000 people who text messaged their opinion to the network, 82 percent gave it to McCain and only 16 percent gave it to Obama.

The Fox TV results demonstrate more than anything else my thesis: what you think of these debates depends on whom you are watching with. While the results of its on-air solicitation for text messages was lopsided in favor of McCain, Fox's focus group of two dozen independents sequestered at "the fabulous Diamond Resorts Polo Towers in Las Vegas" (what's that about?) gave the edge to Obama.

Notes to Myself

My own notes on the debate are instructive for what they don't include — much comment on the issues.

What I noticed first was how scripted both candidates were in their opening remarks. PBS moderator Jim Lehrer urged them both—not once but twice—to "say it directly to him." Obama took heed. As the evening progressed, he directed his remarks more and more to "John." But McCain continued to use the formal Senator Obama until, in an awkward retort to Obama's convention speech, he called him "you" as in "You don't get it."

Lehrer segmented out the 90 minutes into nine "leading questions " — like innings in a baseball game — so it was easy to keep score. In most instances, they traded stump speech lines like meaningless singles.

On earmarks, McCain said one too many times he is "no Miss Congeniality." On the bailout plan, neither ventured too deeply into detail (although if you live on Main Street, they are now your new best friends.)

Lehrer did not get around to foreign policy — the announced topic of this debate — until 40 minutes in. He started with a "leading question" on Iraq. No surprises here in the answers. Except . . . an image begins to form in my mind of The Maverick vs. Mr. Cool. McCain is getting combative, straining to demonstrate his experience in too much detail, irked that his opponent won't respond in kind.

On Afghanistan and Pakistan, they separate themselves out further by style and approach. Obama offers a global view of strategy versus tactics, McCain harks back to his record in Lebanon, Bosnia, Somalia . . . and suddenly he seems very old.

On negotiating with Iran, McCain calls for a "League of Democracies" to deal with Iran. It sounds too much like President Bush's "Coalition of The Willing" in Iraq with ominous overtones of another war in the making.

The maverick is clearly itching for a fight. But Obama counters by discussing negotiation as a tool of diplomacy and weaving in other current trouble areas like North Korea, and seems very worldly and presidential as he does.

At this point, I am riveted to the split-screen shot on TV. McCain vents and Obama listens. In all the many words that will pass between them this fall, this is the Nixon/Kennedy moment. Old vs. new encapsulated in a TV image.

As if the visuals weren't clear enough, McCain pounces on the North Korea opening — and blows it: "As far as North Korea is concerned, our secretary of state, Madeleine Albright, went to North Korea. By the way, North Korea is the most repressive and brutal regime probably on earth. The average South Korean is three inches taller than the average North Korean."

Three inches taller? What's that about?

Closing Statements

Closing statements are as scripted as opening remarks, but after 90 minutes of back and forth, they are a good indicator of how well each candidate has weathered the storm. McCain's turned out to be a jumble of thoughts he wished he had gotten in before. Obama's was smooth as glass.

MCCAIN: I've been involved, as I mentioned to you before, in virtually every major national security challenge we've faced in the last 20-some years. There are some advantages to experience, and knowledge, and judgment.

And I — and I honestly don't believe that Senator Obama has the knowledge or experience and has made the wrong judgments in a number of areas, including his initial reaction to the Russian invasion — aggression in Georgia, to his — you know, we've seen this stubbornness before in this administration to cling to a belief that somehow the surge has not succeeded and failing to acknowledge that he was wrong about the surge is — shows to me that we — that — that we need more flexibility in a president of the United States than that.

OBAMA: Well, let me just make a closing point. You know, my father came from Kenya. That's where I get my name. And in the '60s, he wrote letter after letter to come to college here in the United States because the notion was that there was no other country on earth where you could make it if you tried. The ideals and the values of the United States inspired the entire world.

I don't think any of us can say that our standing in the world now, the way children around the world look at the United States, is the same. And part of what we need to do, what the next president has to do — and this is part of our judgment, this is part of how we're going to keep America safe — is to — to send a message to the world that we are going to invest in issues like education, we are going to invest in issues that — that relate to how ordinary people are able to live out their dreams.

LEHRER: And that ends this debate tonight.

The Talk of Pepe's

After the debate, I went down to Pepe's to buy some smokes. The little corner grocery at the end of the block is run by three brothers from Iraq who came to the United States in the 1980s as Assyrian Christian exiles. They were all great supporters of the Iraq invasion. The eldest is there now working as an interpreter for U.S. troops. The youngest, Bill, was behind the counter.

"So who won?" I asked.

"You mean the Muslim or the old guy?" he asked. "I think your Muslim beat him but there's still time for my guy to come back."

"You can't come back from being old," I said. I asked Bill if he was going to watch the next vice-presidential debate.

"Who's playing?"

"Sarah Palin and Joe Biden," I said.

"Oh her. Yeah, I like her. She's hot. Hey, you should come down and watch with us. We'll make a party of it."

"No thanks," I said, "I think I'll just watch alone."

Down in The Mud

October 10, 2008

On the day John McCain and Barack Obama met for their second presidential debate, the Dow Jones average dropped another 500 points on Wall Street, the Gallup Poll reported a record-low nine percent of Americans have confidence the country is on the right track, and debate moderator Brian Williams took note before introducing the candidates that "politics took an ugly turn on the campaign trail today."

In Clearwater, Florida, Sarah Palin pressed her case that Obama "palled around" with domestic terrorists and "is not a man who sees America the way you and I see America."

Before she did, 3,000 fans waiting for her arrival jeered the press corps accompanying her. When she blamed Katie Couric for her "less-than-successful interview with the kinda mainstream media," they turned on the reporters,

October 9

Dow drops 679 points

October 10

McCain chastens hostile crowd to "be respectful" of Obama

waving thunder sticks and shouting abuse. One loudly shouted a racial slur at an African-American soundman and told him "Sit down, boy."

In Albuquerque, New Mexico, McCain rallied the troops by questioning "Who is the real Barack Obama?" and attacking his opponent on the Fannie Mae takeover, taxes and health care with charges Larry Rohter, of the *New York Times*, flatly stated "contained inaccuracies or exaggerations of his own position or Obama's."

One example: McCain charged Obama praised subprime mortgages as "a good idea" when Obama's full quote was: "Subprime lending started off as a good idea helping Americans buy homes who couldn't previously afford to . . . (but) as certain lenders and brokers began to see how much money could be made, they began to lower their standards. Some appraisers began inflating their estimates to get the deals done. Some borrowers started claiming income they didn't have just to qualify for the loans, and some were engaging in irresponsible speculation."

Meanwhile, back in the Chicago headquarters of the Obama campaign, Democratic strategists were unveiling a

13-minute Internet "documentary" — filled with ominous music and dark imagery — about McCain's links to Charles Keating, a key player in the savings & loan scandal 19 years ago, and corruption charges on which McCain was chastened by Senate colleagues but ultimately exonerated.

"I'm not going to be the first to throw a punch, but I am going to be the last," Obama said in his defense.

On the Airwaves

The two presidential campaigns together are now spending $29 million a week on television commercials, according to the Wisconsin Advertising Project. Nearly 100 percent of McCain's ads and one out of every three of Obama's are negative attacks on their opponent — and some are egregious distortions bordering on flat-out lies.

McCain is particularly guilty (and ham-handed) in this regard. One TV spot now running ("Dishonorable") clips the front and back off an Obama speech to claim Obama "says our troops in Afghanistan are 'just air-raiding villages and killing civilians.' How dishonorable."

The actual quote from an August, 2007, speech was "Now you have narco drug lords who are helping to finance the Taliban . . . so we've got to get the job done there [in Afghanistan], and that requires us to have enough troops that we are not just air raiding villages, and killing civilians, which is causing enormous problems there."

In context, Obama was not criticizing the troops but an administration policy that, according to the *Associated Press*, left the U.S. responsible for more civilian casualties than the insurgents.

This problem was subsequently acknowledged by President Bush, Secretary of Defense Robert Gates and Afghan President Hamid Karzai. No less an authority than Gen. David McKiernan, currently in charge of U.S. troops in Afghanistan, told a Newseum audience last week the number of civilian casualties was hurting U.S. counterinsurgency efforts there.

"We take great measures to try to avoid civilian casualties. But when a mistake is made and inadvertently there is a loss of civilian life unintentionally, we try to make sure that we get out with the truth as quickly as we can," he said.

McKiernan showed a slide of himself meeting with tribal leaders in an Afghan village that had been inadvertently bombed. "That fellow sitting in the middle of the picture there, he lost seven members of his family. Yet he came and talked to me that day, allowed me to apologize to him . . . I don't think that would happen in our country, in the United States of America. I don't think someone that lost seven members of their family would come sit down with somebody in the military and even have a discussion."

In other ads, the McCain campaign insinuates there is something sinister in

Obama's relationship with Mayor Daley's brother Bill (the former Commerce Secretary and Al Gore's 2000 campaign manager) and that Frank Raines, the former head of Fannie Mae, is an Obama advisor when, in fact, they met only once two years ago at a party.

This is a far cry from the John McCain who said last March after the Rev. Jeremiah Wright became an issue in the Democratic primary, "I think that when people support you, it doesn't mean that you support everything they say . . . I know, for example, that I've had endorsements of some people that I didn't share their views but they endorsed me. And so I think we've got to be very careful about that part."

Sewage

Joe Klein, the respected *Time* columnist who has written extensively and often favorably in the past about McCain, posted an item in *Time*'s Swampland political blog the other day decrying the "sewage" now floating about 28 days before the November elections:

"I'm of two minds about how to deal with the McCain campaign's further descent into ugliness. Their strategy is simple: you throw crap against a wall and then giggle as the media try to analyze the putrescence in a way that conveys a sense of balance: 'Well, it is bull-pucky, but the splatter pattern is interesting...'" he wrote.

"I really don't want to be a part of that. Every so often, we journalists have a duty to remind readers just how dingy the McCain campaign, and its right-wing acolytes in the media (I'm looking at you, Sean Hannity) have become."

"Other campaigns have decided that their only shot is going negative, but usually they don't announce it, as several McCain

aides have in recent days — there's no way we can win on the economy, so we're going to go sludge-diving," he continued (listing two more pages of examples).

"I don't want to give currency to this sewage, so it will remain below the fold. And I'll try to devote the lion's share of my time to the issues . . . that should define this campaign. But what a desperate empty embarrassment the McCain campaign has become."

Where Did We Go Wrong?

All the civil rules of politics — the guidelines of truth that once prevented mutually-assured destruction — are out the window. We have this year not one isolated group like the Swift Boat Veterans for Truth slinging mud outside the usual party channels, but whole armadas of dirt dishers cruising a new media ocean called the Internet.

There was concern early in this campaign that the ubiquity of YouTube and a new wave of citizen bloggers would sooner or later unearth some kind of surprise that would change the race, some "Macaca moment" like the one that brought down George Allen in his Virginia Senate race against Jim Webb. And there have been some: The Rev. Wright's fiery speeches, the *Huntington*

Post blog item on Obama's San Francisco fundraiser where he lamented bitter people clinging to their guns and religion.

But the Internet is less a source of surprise this year than common gossip, a babbling bubble machine spewing out so many versions of the truth you can pick and choose which ones you want to believe. Readers gravitate to blogs that share their political persuasion (just as TV news junkies gravitate to cable news channels, Fox or MSNBC, Sean Hannity or Keith Olbermann.) Campaigns feed their favorites with quickie videos and links to stories that denigrate the opposition. And blog followers find themselves with so much grist to process at their own mill they have little appetite to look elsewhere for conflicting opinions.

This race has in many ways been over-covered. It's been sliced and diced in so many ways, by so many people, so constantly, the candidate's positions have been turned into minced meat. As a result, McCain campaign manager Rick Davis's prediction last September that this election will not be about issues but "about a composite view of what people take away from these candidates" is unfortunately coming true.

Once again, the technology of the Internet is racing ahead of the political system's ability to digest it, so forces we don't yet understand are helping shape that composite view.

I receive every few days a forwarded email from a friend with a salacious picture of Sarah Palin in a bikini, a letter from a Wasilla high school classmate who thought she was stuck up, a diatribe from an Obama supporter who thought John McCain acted like a jerk when they were on vacation in the Fiji Islands 13 years ago — and daily clippings from my father, a McCain supporter, about Obama's secret Muslim connections.

When I went to print out a *Washington Post* story on Palin's Clearwater appearance, I found 161 pages of "comments" (1,564) attached—all posted less than 24 hours after the story was written. It used to be only the debates had spin rooms. Now every story printed has one.

A Sub-prime Crisis in Journalism

We have a sub-prime crisis in journalism. The barriers to entry are so low and the opportunities to express yourself so vast that political discourse is now a muddle of half-baked opinions finally free of what Sarah Palin calls "the media filter."

But it may well be that what we need now more than ever is a media filter. For better or worse, the mainstream media in the past was constrained by space (and editors) to tightly packaged synopses of daily campaign events. No more. If you want to know what reporters at the *New York Times*, *Washington Post* or *Time* think of the race, you don't wait for the Sunday think piece. You tune into *The Caucus, Trailings* or *Swampland* — several times a day — for their online updates.

Reporters covering the race have been reduced to the status of just another blogger. This is a shame because there are more good reporters on the campaign trail this year than any race I can remember.

The fact checking they provide, the transcripts they post on their websites and background material on candidates and their finances is more extensive than ever (now that they have the tools and space afforded by the Internet.) But their authority as writers of the truth is diminished — in no small way by the ability of the campaigns to use that same Internet to go over their heads directly to the people.

What Sarah Palin demonstrates every day that she avoids answering questions from the press is how little regard she has for their role as guardians of the truth — or the service they provide. Whether that is wise or foolish will be seen on Election Day.

There is an emerging consensus based on poll trends that barring some October surprise Barack Obama will win the presidency. There are any number of likely reasons he will: the depressed economy, the human and financial costs of the Iraq War or simple Bush fatigue.

As remarkable as this would be in the history of America, the symbol of this fall campaign is not Obama but Palin, who reads everything that is put in front of her, but can't actually remember what she read. Ain't that a sign of the times?

Joe for President

October 17, 2008

THE BEST LINE in the last presidential debate didn't come from either candidate but from George Will afterward on ABC. "If the winner of this debate is the next president of the United States, the next president of the United States will be Joe The Plumber."

The debate spanned a period of 90 minutes and seemed at times like a political boxing match. John McCain threw all the punches and Barack Obama played a masterful game of rope-a-dope. But it was Joe The Plumber, mentioned 20 times in the course of the evening, who stole the show.

And he wasn't even there. Joe Wurzelbacher (whom McCain incorrectly called Wurzelberger) was back home in Holland, Ohio, where until last Sunday he lived a life of quiet obscurity.

It was just last Sunday that he ran into Obama on the campaign trail and engaged in a spirited debate over Obama's plan to raise taxes on people making over $250,000. Joe

October 11

Obama meets Joe the Plumber in Ohio

October 13

U.S. takes stake in bailout banks

Dow gains 936 points

October 15

Last presidential debate, McCain cites Joe The Plumber 20 times

Dow drop 733 points

complained that if he buys his boss's plumbing company, he'll fall in that category, and Obama replied, "It's not that I want to punish your success, it's just that I want to make sure that everybody who is behind you, that they've got a chance to have success too. I think when you spread the wealth around, it's good for everybody."

The exchange has been bandied about on right wing talk radio ever since. Fox News boiled it down to a Marxist catchphrase — "spread the wealth around" — and overlayed the rest of the video with outraged commentary, including a telephone interview with Wurzelbacher who said he resented the way he was treated. "Robin Hood stole from greedy rich people and redistributed it to the peasants, so to speak, so if he's calling us peasants, I kind of resent that." And that might have been the end of Joe's 15 minutes of fame.

But McCain wasn't going to let it go. He opened Wednesday's debate with a slightly embellished version of Joe The Plumber's struggle [he is not a licensed plumber and his boss was unaware of his desire to buy the company] and tailored the rest of his answers to all the Joe The Plumbers out there (at least, those who are making $250,000 a year.)

"He worked 10, 12 hours a day. And he wanted to buy the business, " McCain said, "but he looked at your tax plan and saw that he was going to pay much higher taxes. You were going to put him in a higher tax bracket, which was going to increase his taxes, which was going to cause him not to be able to employ people, while Joe was trying to realize the American dream.

"Joe, I want to tell you," McCain said mugging to the camera, "I'll not only help you buy that business that you worked your whole life for — I'll keep your taxes low and I'll provide available and affordable health care for you and your employees."

Strong Start, Weak Finish

It was a strong start for a candidate who has been struggling to find a message for his campaign. Republicans who wanted to see McCain get more aggressive in his attacks on Obama were pleased. "I wanted to see the fighter pilot come out, and that's what I saw tonight," Bill Bennett, one of the CNN Republican consultants, glowed afterward. But somewhere in the middle of McCain's derring do, when moderator Bob Schieffer asked the candidates to comment on the nasty tone out on the campaign trail, his feistiness turned to petulance.

He treated the debate as if it were a dogfight, flitting around from one detail in Obama's record to another (and repeating charges fact-checkers have found untrue), darting around from energy policy to trade pacts to drug lords in Columbia who are killing our children (all in one question), and making sure he always got the last word. When he wasn't talking, he was grimacing. When he wasn't grimacing, he was shrugging his shoulders or raising an eyebrow at his opponent's answers. Perhaps one too many times.

Joe The Plumber, like Sarah Palin, was another one of those fighter pilot surprises McCain likes to throw into the fray, but, like Palin, the surprise wore thin.

CNN ran a graph under the debate showing the instant responses of men and women in a focus group of undecided voters in Ohio. Consistently, women responded less favorably to the attacks than men. When McCain defended Sarah Palin's readiness to become president, the women flat-lined while men curiously agreed. But many of McCain's best attack lines drew little response from either.

Two instant polls after the debate told the story. McCain scored more hits, but Obama won the debate. CNN found 58 percent of watchers thought Obama won and only 31 percent gave the debate to McCain. CBS polled a sample of uncommitted voters where 53 percent gave it to Obama, 22 percent to McCain, and 24 percent called it a draw.

October 16

Oil prices fall below $70 a barrel

October 19

Former Secretary of State Colin Powell endorses Obama

October 22

Reports show Republicans bought Sarah Palin $150,000 wardrobe for the campaign

Not His Best, But Good Enough

The Barack Obama who took the stage Wednesday had everything to lose and nothing to gain by getting into an argument with McCain, and he acted like it. He had his talking points, and he delivered them in a direct and serious manner.

But he seemed unprepared for some of the issues McCain raised — that was one of the reasons McCain raised them — and stupefied by others. The plight of Joe The Plumber didn't really register in his mind as a critical debate topic until after McCain used Joe two or three more times as the stand-in for Everyman. Finally, Obama too started talking to Joe through the camera, as in "Joe, I'm not going to fine you" if the company doesn't offer health care insurance.

Aside from correcting the record, however, Obama showed little interest in engaging. He ceded the last word on many subjects to McCain and looked plaintively at Schieffer for the next question.

Last Sunday, Andrew Sullivan wrote a piece in the *London Times* about Obama's ability to remain unruffled under the most trying circumstances:

"His calm is almost unnatural. I've been following Barack Obama closely now for two years and I've never seen him or even heard of him losing his temper," Sullivan wrote.

"He lollops along with a calm smile and a physical fluency that is hard to mock or copy. If he were a boxer, he'd be the kind who keeps moving but hangs back. He waits for his opponents to take a swing, ducks and comes back into the game. He sticks to a game plan and rarely deviates. And he waits for his opponent to

make an error. Watching his autumn fight with McCain reminds me of the Wile E Coyote and Road Runner cartoons. Every elaborate attempt to blow Obama up leaves his opponents with sooty faces and a trail of smoke rising from the tops of their heads."

That was the Obama who showed up.

The Upper Hand

It is said that Barack Obama has gained the upper hand in the race. The events of the last 20 days in the financial markets have certainly skewed the election against any Republican, and McCain showed during the debate that even when he throws his best punch, he is powerless to stem the tide for change.

Holding the upper hand gives Obama many moves that are denied to McCain. He can pick and choose his targets over the next 20 days, focusing in on the narrowing group of undecideds in states where they will make a difference. McCain cannot. He has to make up ground everywhere.

Obama doesn't need to tear down his opponent. He needs to grow his already 50-plus margin in the polls, in effect turning his advantage into a movement. This happens with strong, positive TV spots coming on the air just at that time when voters are weary of all the negatives, and Obama has plenty of money to run them. If McCain tries to follow suit, he'll only solidify his losing base so he has to keep attacking, even if he doesn't have the money for it.

More importantly, the Obama campaign can now unleash the field organization it has been building since those first days in Iowa into an America conditioned by the debates to believe Obama is every bit ready to become the next president. The votes are there; they just need to be harvested.

All those names meticulously gathered over the Internet, at rallies, through text messages and commercial databases, all those field offices he has set up in small towns across America, all those newly registered voters now come into play. The turnout game has begun.

Last week, Obama stopped by one of those field offices in Ohio for a training session of volunteers. As a former community organizer himself, he marveled at the care that has gone into building the field organization. "We've been designing and we've been engineering and we've been at the drawing board and we've been tinkering," he said. "Now it's time to just take it for a drive. Let's see how this baby runs."

Last Shot

Wednesday's debate was McCain's last shot at speaking to an audience of 60 million Americans. He decided to use it to speak to only one, Joe the Plumber. Even that might not have worked out quite the way he planned it.

The *Associated Press* found Wurzelbacher shortly after the debate. He said he found it "surreal" to be at the center of a presidential campaign, but he still wouldn't commit to a candidate. Who's he going to vote for? "That's for me and a button to know."

Celebrate America

October 24, 2008

BARACK OBAMA WAS in St. Louis last Saturday night addressing 100,000 people under The Gateway Arch. John McCain was in North Carolina protecting Joe the Plumber from creeping socialism. Sarah Palin was in New York preparing for her *Saturday Night Live* appearance and I was back home in Chicago in a parish social hall attending a dance to raise money for St. Hedwig's Catholic Church in Bucktown.

St. Hedwig's is not a stop on anybody's campaign trail this year. There was a time back in The Depression when it might have been. That was when its 3,000-member congregation was the largest Polish parish in America. Changing times and increased mobility allowed many of them to move to the suburbs after World War II, opening the way for new generations of Puerto Ricans, Filipinos, Mexicans and now gentrifying whites to put their faith in the 107-year-old cathedral.

That faith is not easy to come by these days. Six months ago, a fire swept through the church basement and burned

October 28

Dow jumps 889 points

up through the floor under the altar belching smoke into the sanctuary. Since the fire, the church has held its services in the school gym while parishioners struggle to find the $3.2 million needed for repairs.

In an era of $700 billion bailout packages for Wall Street, that doesn't seem like much. But for the mostly poor and middle class parishioners it's a mountain of money, and the task of raising it is all the more daunting because St. Hedwig's is not one unified church but three churches in one building. Bucktown is one of those inner city communities that seems to grow a new ethnic skin every couple generations but never casts off the old. So Sunday services at St. Hedwig's are alternately conducted in Polish, Spanish and English by priests specially chosen for their multi-lingual skills.

When In Doubt, Throw a Party

A lot of debate went on in church councils over how much to charge for a ticket to the dance. Too much and no one would come. Too little and nothing would be made. The important thing, they decided, was to get everyone to come together to make a new start.

They settled on $15 at the door, plus $5 for food, $1 for soda and $2 for beer and wine.

There would be two kinds of entertainment. DJ Grezegorz Drden, the Polish Dr. Dre, would spin his eclectic mix of disco waltzes and Elvis oldies while Escorpeonez del Norte, seven men in white suits and cowboy hats, would fill the gaps with music from south of the border.

When my wife and I arrived, we were greeted by Father Stan. He gave my wife a warm hug since he recognized her from Sunday services and offered me a cold handshake since he didn't. The gym was decorated with 30 red balloons tied to chairs. The food was set out on tables along one wall, heaps of food tended by women in party dresses holding serving spoons over aluminum roasting pans. There was pulled pork and pierogi, Spanish rice and egg rolls, tamales next to goulash, beef sate beside Filipino noodles, and more salad and dessert combinations than I can name.

On the gymnasium stage, where the priests usually put the cross and flowers during Sunday services, the band was setting up. DJ Drden brought his own flashing red, green and yellow gobo lights and smoke machine, and pretty soon people got up to dance.

The first couple on the floor were two 75-year-old Polish women in floor length skirts traversing the floor in formal waltz step. A young blond and her husband soon joined them, then an elderly Mexican couple, a mother with two young children, and a priest with a young Filipino woman. The spacious gym, half empty when we arrived, swelled with people and more lined up at the door to get in.

We sat at a table with neighbors we knew only from passing in the street: Ralph and Beverly Esposito, who have been teachers at the local public elementary school since 1968; two women who said they have lived in the neighborhood for 50 years; Jesse and Gladys Barrera, best known for their annual contribution to the 4th of July fireworks display in the alley behind the Diazes.

As the crowds poured in, teenagers rushed to set up more tables. But there were not enough tables. When one couple rose to dance, another sat down to eat.

Hundreds came that night to celebrate the rebirth of a church. And through the whole evening, no one mentioned John McCain or Barack Obama, Sarah Palin or Joe Biden. No one talked about their 401(k), foreclosed mortgages, job layoffs or Joe the Plumber's tax liability, and no one really believes a change in Washington will trickle down much into the neighborhood.

As they laughed and danced, what they all knew is that if the church is to be saved, they will have to do it themselves — together.

Ohio The Battleground State

October 31, 2008

DEFIANCE, OHIO — Karri Krendl usually does not sleep with a gun at her side.

She usually doesn't sleep out in her Chevy Suburban either, listening for her mule to bray or her pony to act up. But ever since she painted her barn with an Obama "Hope" insignia that has been her life.

Karri lives with her husband Dan on a farm Krendl's grandfather bought in 1920 outside Spencerville, a rural community of about 2,500 people in northwest Ohio. Karri, 51, is a family physician and Dan, 50, is a science teacher at Spencerville High School. Both are unabashed Democrats. Most of their neighbors are not.

Last summer, when she heard the Obama campaign was looking to paint a few "Barns for Obama" to establish a beachhead in this largely Republican area, she was one of the first to sign up. The campaign sent an artist up from Cincinnati to map out the design. Dan rented a lift and, with the help of about a dozen friends and relatives, they

October 31

Obama returns to Iowa for one last speech; 70,000 supporters turn out

November 1

McCain makes final appearance on *Saturday Night Live*

began to paint. They painted almost 24 hours straight. After nightfall, Dan set up some lights and they kept painting. The next day, they held a picnic to celebrate. Democrats from miles around — about 60 in all — came to add the final touches.

Karri could not have been prouder. "It's really a symbol of unity, a way to let other people know there are Obama supporters around here and that we're a positive presence in the community," she said. Not everyone shared her excitement.

The next Sunday, Karri and Dan went out for a bike ride. Turning around to admire their handiwork, they saw "NIGER LOVER" spray-painted across the barn. ("It turns out racists are not especially good spellers," said Dan.) They quietly repaired the damage.

A week later, they went to the Spencerville High School homecoming. When they returned, they found green paint splashed over the barn and "Nobama" scrawled across it. Whoever did it also left gaping tire tracks spun in donuts across their lawn. Again, they repainted.

Two weeks ago, Karri and Dan got another scare. The sheriff pulled into the driveway to warn them that over in the next town vandals had just doused two Obama signs hung on the barn of Gwen Picer with gasoline, but were driven off before they could light it. That's when Dan pulled out the rifle.

"We live on a farm. Of course, we have a gun," Dan said calmly. "Would I ever shoot at someone? I doubt it. But you have to take these threats serious."

In Ohio, people take their politics serious.

The View from Bud's Restaurant

"If you're going to be successful in Ohio, you have to remember two things," an Obama field organizer told me. "People in Ohio hate robocalls, and people in Ohio love their yard signs."

Driving into Defiance along route 15, I could see what he meant. Every other house had an Obama or McCain-Palin sign. It didn't matter whether it was a farmhouse set out in the cornfields or white clapboard houses lined up one after another in the small towns, there was a sign in the yard for one politician or another, and often many.

At Bud's Restaurant the talk at the counter was about who was stealing whose signs. The day before, there had been a letter to the editor in the Defiance *Crescent News* complaining about sign theft. Everyone at the counter had a story about signs stolen in the night. One girl who had an Obama sign in her front yard complained of a neighbor who, seeing it, painted McCain-Palin in letters three times as large across his adjoining fence.

"You'll find it's mostly Republicans around here, but there's a lot more Obama activity than I've seen before," Rita the waitress noted. "They've got offices all over the place and it's making this election . . . very interesting."

The Battleground State

Indeed, this swath of small towns and rural farms in western Ohio is at the eye of the storm in one of this year's most hotly contested states. In 2004, while John Kerry was rolling up huge numbers in Cleveland, Toledo and other industrial cities, George Bush swept through rural Ohio rolling up 2-1 and 3-1 margins in the small towns, and building a 118,000 plurality that gave the Republicans Ohio, and ultimately the presidency.

Kerry had largely ignored the western region of the state. Conservative social values on abortion, guns and gay marriage make it rough terrain for any Democrat. But the Obama campaign is not ceding any ground this year. They have opened 81 field offices in the state, over 50 of them in small towns and rural communities. This time around, they are moving in to stay.

The Obama canvassing effort is called "Neighbor to Neighbor." The local field directors are paid staff who have all gone through an intensive community organizing workshop called "Obama Camp." Their mission is not only to establish an Obama presence in these communities, but to build a network of local volunteers who will stay on after the election to build the Democratic party.

"They've invested in a civic infrastructure on a scale that has never happened," Marshall Ganz, a labor organizer who worked with César Chávez's farmworker movement and led some of those sessions, told the *Washington Post.* The implications, he added, are "profound."

With its huge financial advantage and sophisticated Internet operation, the Obama campaign has trained thousands of new Democratic volunteers, organized them into teams with captains and foot soldiers, and given them an array of Internet tools to search out, find out and turn out Obama voters.

"The basic concept is not a new or revolutionary one," says Jon Carson, Obama's national field director. "Campaigns have always wanted to have a grass-roots, volunteer-driven effort. The two pieces that came together for us . . . was the sheer volume of the people who wanted to get involved and the technology making it easier than ever before to find us. It wasn't that Democrats didn't get it" in past campaigns. "It was that . . . they weren't able to make it work on this scale."

A Scattershot Approach

In 2004, the Democratic approach to organizing was scattershot. While Kerry focused on delivering the campaign message at rallies and in his TV ads, his Get Out The Vote campaign was left to independent 527 committees like Americans Coming Together (ACT) and MoveOn. Org. In part, this was a way for Democrats to get around federal spending limits by assigning certain tasks to "uncoordinated" independent entities.

In Ohio, ACT brought more than 200,000 new Democrats to the polls by pounding the streets, and MoveOn.org came up with a clever internet-based way for committed volunteers to download call lists and track responses from home. But there was no easy way to integrate their efforts or, like the Republicans, tie into consumer databases to find likely new voters. So when the election was over, the Ohio Democratic Party tried to remedy the problem by creating a software program called "Vote Builder" and used it in 2006 to help elect Gov. Ted Strickland and Sen. Sherrod Brown.

Vote Builder provided a foundation, but it wasn't long before the Internet team at Obama headquarters was souping it up with blogs, Facebook connections and other social networking twists.

MyBarackObama.com

The blueprint for the Obama field organizing effort is laid out in a website called MyBarackObama.com (nickname: my.BO). It is a 2.0 version of "Vote Builder" that Obama's technology gurus developed, by trial and error, throughout the primary process.

From a user standpoint, it is the Swiss watch of campaign organizing, elegant and easy to navigate. If you sign up and type in your zip code, you can find nearby campaign events, download lists of voters to call from home on your own time, get maps with the names of voters targeted as potential supporters, send out private fund-raising appeals, and create your own blog to share your personal experiences on the campaign trail or build team morale.

After calling or canvassing, you then upload the results back to the Obama website. The feedback is instantaneous. Last week in Ohio, for instance, Chicago headquarters knows that volunteers knocked on 340,846 doors last weekend and made 394,335 phone calls. They have already sorted the names and addresses of voters who favor or lean toward Obama into an Election Day call list, flushed out the names of voters who don't, and created a fresh contact list for next week.

If a canvasser runs across an undecided voter, the voter might be added to the new list (with comments on his reservations). The contact list is then salted with new prospects culled from the consumer databases Obama gained access to when he shifted the Democratic party operations to Chicago last summer. These databases include thousands of mailing lists for car buyers, magazine subscribers, sports fans, opera buffs, gun owners, etc.

Using predictive models, the campaign searches out names and addresses of people "likely to vote Democratic" — Volvo buyers, New Yorker subscribers or Sierra Club contributors, for instance — for volunteers to visit.

But the software is only half the story. "Neighbor to Neighbor" is where the Obama campaign puts a human face on the Internet operation. It does this by getting volunteers to share their own reasons for supporting Obama (and, of course, providing scripts of talking points if anyone comes up short.) Even after voter responses have been categorized and uploaded, volunteers are encouraged to discuss them in the field offices or share them in future training sessions.

Defiance, Ohio

In a former print shop turned Obama headquarters in Defiance, Caleb Finkenbiner, 29, is instructing new volunteers on how to canvass. They are going into the Republican side of town, but they are not literally walking door-to-door. They have maps generated at Obama headquarters that identify specific houses, and specific voters, Obama headquarters wants them to contact this week. "They do the voodoo[1] that they do up in headquarters, and I'm grateful for what they do," the field organizer tells me. "But it doesn't mean anything until we actually go knock on doors."

In addition to canvassing, the Obama office today is running a test of its Election Day drill. (The same drill was practiced at offices across the state last week.) On Election Day, volunteers are expected to come in at specific times of the day for specific tasks. In the morning, the task is calling lists of supporters who haven't voted early. Around noon, poll sheets will be reviewed to check off who has. By late afternoon, supporters who haven't voted will be tracked down and escorted to the polls.

Defiance is not inherently friendly territory for Obama. In 2004, Bush beat Kerry there by 24 percentage points, but it is a small universe of voters. Only 18,000 of the 27,000 registered voters in Defiance County went to the polls in 2004. 11,500 voted for Bush and 6,700 voted for Kerry. If 1,000 fewer Republicans show up this Tuesday and the Obama field office can gin up 3,000 more supporters, Obama might actually win Defiance County.

"That would be my dream," the field organizer said, "to have Chuck Todd (on MSNBC) pull up the map on Election Night and say, 'look what happened here in tiny Defiance, Ohio.' I think a lot of people are going to be surprised."(2)

Meanwhile, Back On The Farm

In spite of the ongoing threat of vandalism, Karri Krendl is hopeful. "We brought a lot of people out of the woodwork," she says. "If there are 20 Democratic votes in Spencerville, that's a good year. This year I think we'll have a few more. People are tired of this divisiveness. They want something more."

Her hope — the hope she painted on her barn — is that Obama can restore a more civil tone to American politics.

"After the vandalism, one of my medical colleagues asked if I wasn't afraid we'll have more of this — more of these racist, angry people stepping forward to harm us — if Obama is elected," she says. "What worries me more is if what will happen if Obama loses."

"Let's say we do win the Iraq war, and all the soldiers come home . . . and there are no jobs. We'll have college kids who can't afford college, people out of work and a very militaristic culture in charge. Where is the racist anger going to go then? If you look at where the Republicans have led us, we have a wider gap between the rich and the poor than ever, and no jobs, and I'm afraid there may be class warfare on our own soil . . . and America will be a mess."

---

(1) In the last stages of the campaign, Obama tech gurus at headquarters came up with a mobile phone software program they called 'Houdini', *Newsweek* reported after the election. Poll watchers with Houdini installed on their cellphones would call in the names of Obama supporters as soon as they appeared at the polls. These names would then be automatically deleted from call lists used by volunteers back at the field offices. The program cut about three hours off the Election Day response time and, as the end of voting approached, made it easier to target voters who had not yet gone to the polls.

(2) The final results in Defiance County were McCain: 9,334 (54%), Obama 7,394 (43%). A net gain for the Democrats of 13 percentage points over 2004.

End of Story . . . Start to Change

November 7, 2008

CHANGE IS NOT a light switch. You can't just turn it on and off. It's easy to promise, hard to effect, and recognizable only in retrospect after experience decides whether it has been for the better or worse.

Twenty months after putting change on the national agenda, Barack Obama woke up Wednesday morning with a sweeping mandate to give it his best shot. He won the presidency with a larger share of the popular vote than any Democratic president since Lyndon Johnson in 1964. He takes office with his Democratic party firmly in control of both the House and the Senate, his vanquished opponent holding out the olive branch of "earnest efforts to help him bring us together," and a country embroiled in two wars and on the precipice of the worst financial crisis since the Great Depression.

He succeeds a president who came into office only after a Supreme Court battle over hanging chads in Florida, who

November 4

Election Day

Popular Vote Results:

Obama 69,456,884 (52.9%)
McCain 59,934,813 (45.7%)

Electoral College:

Obama 365
McCain 173

Campaign Costs:

Obama $740 million
McCain $347 million

Cost Per Vote:

Obama $10.65
McCain $ 5.78

Total Spending (all candidates)

$1.7 billion

was re-elected by virtue of guttersnipe attacks on his opponent's Vietnam war record, and who leaves office with the lowest approval rating of any president in history and 85 percent of the electorate believing America is on the wrong track.

The question is not whether Obama will change Washington. New administrations bring with them new people and new policies that inevitably set a new agenda. Obama's is a middle class tax cut, national health care and major investments in alternative energy, education and infrastructure. But he inherits a $700 billion bailout package that could leave him with a trillion dollar deficit in his first year in office, and an economy that is in a tailspin toward depression.

The question is whether — "in the fierce urgency of now" — he can accomplish any of this and at the same time fulfill his campaign promise to change the way Washington does business. Curtailing the influence of lobbyists, making the legislative process more transparent and fighting the entrenched interests requires a slow evolution in the Washington culture that will pit him against some of his own party leaders.

Call me a cynic, but winning the presidency was a cakewalk compared to the dance that will be required to change Washington *and* pass his programs.

Total Victory

Obama's victory was complete. In the parlance of a horse race he hit the trifecta, putting together an impressive combination of money, mechanics and message.

He raised an astonishing $740 million — more than $300 million of it from Internet contributions averaging $86 apiece — and he spent it taking his message to parts of the country that haven't seen a serious Democratic presidential contender in 30 years. His campaign married new age technologies to old school community organizing and fielded a professional and volunteer operation in 18 battleground states that brought 12 of them into his victory column (ten more than John Kerry won in 2004).

His organization set a new standard for presidential campaigns. At the next Republican convention, Rudy Giuliani will have to look elsewhere for his laugh lines before he again questions what a community organizer does. The Internet-based field operation the Obama team put together has taken American politics to a new level of sophistication, and it's doubtful we can ever climb back down.

"Ice Cold Discipline"

In their *New York Times* election wrap-up, Adam Nagourney, Jim Rutenberg and Jeff Zeleny found an admirer in McCain's own campaign manager, Steve Schmidt.

The Obama campaign, Schmidt told the *Times*, "was perfectly run; it made few mistakes. And it took full advantage of an environment where the American people had turned on the incumbent president of the Republican Party and badly wanted change."

Obama himself, Schmidt added, "was a once-in-a-generation orator. A good debater. And (he had) an eloquent message. He was . . . ice cold disciplined about the execution of his campaign message. He was an extremely formidable candidate."

Obama, The Candidate

The principal reason Obama won, however, was the candidate himself. In presidential politics, authenticity is a great American virtue, and we reward it with our vote regardless of race, creed, or gender (see Sarah Palin.) John McCain failed in his quest for the presidency because he ran a campaign that was not in his nature. George Bush won because he did.

Barack Obama is a complex man living inside a complex skin. The experiences that shaped him over the course of his life are so wide ranging it took him two books to describe them. But he used that writing to find a way of speaking that reflects his depth of thought in terms ordinary people can easily understand. When he speaks, you feel you are touching his core values. Whether you agree with him or not, you don't feel lied to. Under the tutelage of his friend and advisor David Axelrod, he has also learned how valuable it is in politics to distill his message into a few sentences — even better, a single word. Change.

Change is the oldest mantra in the political vocabulary. But in Obama's eloquent hands it became a punctuation mark on simple ideas simply expressed. As did "Hope" and "Yes We Can." True believers at his speeches waited for his pauses to shout these punch lines back at him. But it is what Obama said between the pauses that won him the presidency. He made sense of a senselessly complex world that most of America think is stacked against them.

Grant Park

About the time the TV networks showed Ohio and Florida trending Democratic, I threw on my tennies Election Night and hopped the Blue Line down to Grant Park. The closer the train got to the Loop, the larger the crowds were on the platform. Although less than a quarter of the one million people Mayor Daley predicted turned out, the 240,000 who did were nothing to sneeze at. The ticketed and the ticket-less flowed peacefully along the sidewalks and closed-off streets to find some vantage point to catch a glimpse of the next president.

Access to the park was divided into areas of influence. Funders and key supporters, brought in on trolleys from the nearby Hyatt Regency, ringed the front of the stage.

The general public crowded in behind. The media observed from television risers, trailers and press tents (if they paid the fee) or a general press section with big TV's (if they did not). I occupied the latter along with a number of Columbia College students, foreign press reporters, Richard Roeper, Citizen Kate, and Amarosa from "The Apprentice."

The historic import of the night was palpable.

"A nation that in living memory struggled violently over racial equality will have as its next president a 47-year-old, one-term U.S. senator born of a Kenyan father and Kansan mother," Mike Dorning and Jim Tankersley wrote the morning after in the *Chicago Tribune*. "He is the first president elected from Chicago and the first to rise from a career in Illinois politics since Abraham Lincoln emerged from frontier obscurity to lead the nation through the Civil War and the abolition of slavery."

A young black man seeing Jesse Jackson slip into the VIP area shouted, "Reverend, you paved the way!" Two longtime black reporters who have been covering Chicago's polarized racial politics since the days of Harold Washington hugged when CNN projected Obama the winner. Two other women at my side broke into uncontrollable sobs.

Looking out into the endless sea of spectators, I could see people crying, dancing, and chanting "Yes We Can." On the Jumbotron, cameras caught the Rev. Jackson with tears welling in his eyes and Oprah Winfrey exuberantly leaning over the rope line. It was a night of cell phone text messages to friends ("I'm here, where r u?") photos for the memory book and souvenirs for the T-shirt drawer or bulletin board.

A Gracious Loser

Meanwhile, at the Biltmore Hotel in Phoenix, the mood was more somber. John McCain stepped to the microphone to offer his concession speech. For the first time in months, the John McCain who captured the imagination a year ago with his promise to reach across the aisle to find solutions to America's problems was back. But it was too late.

The slash and burn tactics brought to his campaign by Karl Rove's team of Republican operatives had taken their toll. The strategy of "energizing the base" — epitomized by the selection of Sarah Palin as his vice-presidential running mate — had been an abject failure. Republican turnout this year was the worst in 30 years. Among new voters going to the polls, Obama beat McCain, 72 percent to 27 percent, according to exit polls.

McCain's floundering attempts to find a compelling message lost him the traditional Republican edge among women and white men. His reversal on his own immigration bill — to accommodate the right wing of his party in the primaries — cost him dearly in Hispanic support in

Florida, Nevada, New Mexico and Colorado, all of which he lost to Obama.

But it was the John McCain of old who took the stage Tuesday night in Phoenix to recognize the historic significance and special pride African-Americans can take in Obama's election. "Let there be no reason now for any American not to cherish their citizenship in this the greatest nation on earth," he said.

"Senator Obama and I have had our differences — and he has prevailed. No doubt those differences remain," he went on. "These are difficult times for our country. And I pledge to him tonight to do all in my power to help him lead us in the many challenges we face. I urge all Americans who supported me to join me in not just congratulating him but offering our next president our goodwill and earnest effort to find ways to come together."

More Than 'Just Words'

Hillary Clinton once scoffed at Obama's speeches as "just words." John McCain called them lofty oratory. But they carry the hope Obama offers America just as much as Franklin Delano Roosevelt's fireside chats did on the radio in 1933. They are the articulation of ideas, and without ideas there can be no change. Delivered by a man who knows what he wants to say, and when he wants to say it, they come with a power we haven't seen since the days of John F. Kennedy.

Obama had a few more things he wanted to say Election Night. The build-up to his appearance was a medley of songs he'd used along the campaign trail: "Signed, Sealed, Delivered" by Stevie Wonder, "Only in America" by Brooks and Dunn, "Sweet Home, Chicago" by Robert Johnson and "Your Love is Lifting Me Higher" by Jackie Wilson. But the only music playing when Obama came out on stage was the sound of 100,000 people cheering.

"If there is anyone out there who still doubts that America is a place where all things are possible; who still wonders if the dream of our founders is alive in our time; who still questions the power of our democracy, tonight is your answer," he began.

"It's the answer that led those who have been told for so long by so many to be cynical, and fearful, and doubtful of what we can achieve to put their hands on the arc of history and bend it once more toward the hope of a better day."

"The road ahead will be long. Our climb will be steep. We may not get there in one year or even one term, but America — I have never been more hopeful than I am tonight that we will get there. I promise you — we as a people will get there.

"There will be setbacks and false starts. There are many who won't agree with every decision or policy I make as president, and we know that government can't solve every problem. But I will always be honest with you about the challenges we face. I will listen to you, especially when we disagree. And above all, I will ask you to join in the work of remaking this nation the only way it's been

done in America for 221 years — block by block, brick by brick, calloused hand by calloused hand."

"And to all those watching tonight from beyond our shores, from parliaments and palaces to those who are huddled around radios in the forgotten corners of our world — our stories are singular, but our destiny is shared, and a new dawn of American leadership is at hand. To those who would tear this world down — we will defeat you. To those who seek peace and security — we support you. And to all those who have wondered if America's beacon still burns as bright — tonight we proved once more that the true strength of our nation comes not from the might of our arms or the scale of our wealth, but from the enduring power of our ideals: democracy, liberty, opportunity and unyielding hope.

"For that is the true genius of America — that America can change."

God bless you, and good luck.

Index

About The Author

STUMP CONNOLLY HAS covered five presidential campaigns as a newspaper reporter, television producer and Internet commentator, and is presently the chief political correspondent of *The Week Behind*. He is the author of two previous campaign books, *STUMP, a Campaign Journal* about the 1996 race and *Talk's Cheap, Let's Race!* about the 2004 campaign, and a co-producer of the 1992 documentary series "Road To The Presidency" *Inside the Clinton Campaign*.

Acknowledgments

IN THE COURSE of the campaign, I've had an opportunity to meet many friends who have made an honorable life in politics. I want to thank them for sharing this experience with me. They include David Axelrod, Richard Buckman, Mike Flannery, Tom Jarman, Karri and Don Krendl, John Kupper, Don Rose, Thom Serafin, Andy Shaw, Roger Simon and Tom Southwick.

I also want to thank Marta Bender, Christy Bowman, Lucy Domino, Bruce Jacobs, Donna LaPietra and Elizabeth Station for their editorial guidance, and Bruce and Lorelei Bendinger at First Flight Books for their assistance with the book part of writing a book.